COLLINS LIVING HISTORY

Black Peoples of the Americas
1500-1900s

Donald Hinds

Series editor: Christopher Culpin

CollinsEducational

An imprint of HarperCollinsPublishers

Contents

UNIT 1   Arriving in the Americas   page   6

UNIT 2   Slavery   16

UNIT 3   Slave resistance   28

UNIT 4   Struggles for freedom   40

UNIT 5   A free people?   48

Glossary   61

Index   63

attainment target 1

Questions aimed at this attainment target find out how much you know and understand about the past. Some questions are about how things were different in history: not only people's food, or clothes but their beliefs too. Others are about how things change through history, sometimes quickly, sometimes slowly, sometimes a little, sometimes a lot. Other questions ask you to explain why things were different in the past, and why changes took place.

attainment target 2

This attainment target is about understanding what people say about the past. Historians, as well as lots of other people, try to describe what the past was like. Sometimes they say different things. This attainment target is about understanding these differences and why they occur.

attainment target 3

This attainment target is about historical sources and how we use them to find out about the past. Some questions are about the historical evidence we can get from sources. Others ask you about how valuable this evidence might be.

Introduction

The picture below shows black slaves working on a sugar plantation in the Caribbean. It was painted by a European artist and there are visual clues in the picture about white attitudes to black people and slavery. You will find out more about these attitudes as you read through this book and look at the sources.

In this book we will discover why African slaves were shipped thousands of kilometres to the Americas, and what life on the plantations was like for them. We will then find out about slaves who managed to escape to freedom, and we will look at some of the famous slave revolts. We will study the lives of black and white men and women who struggled tirelessly to bring slavery to an end. Finally, we will see how much the lives of black people in the Americas changed after slavery was abolished.

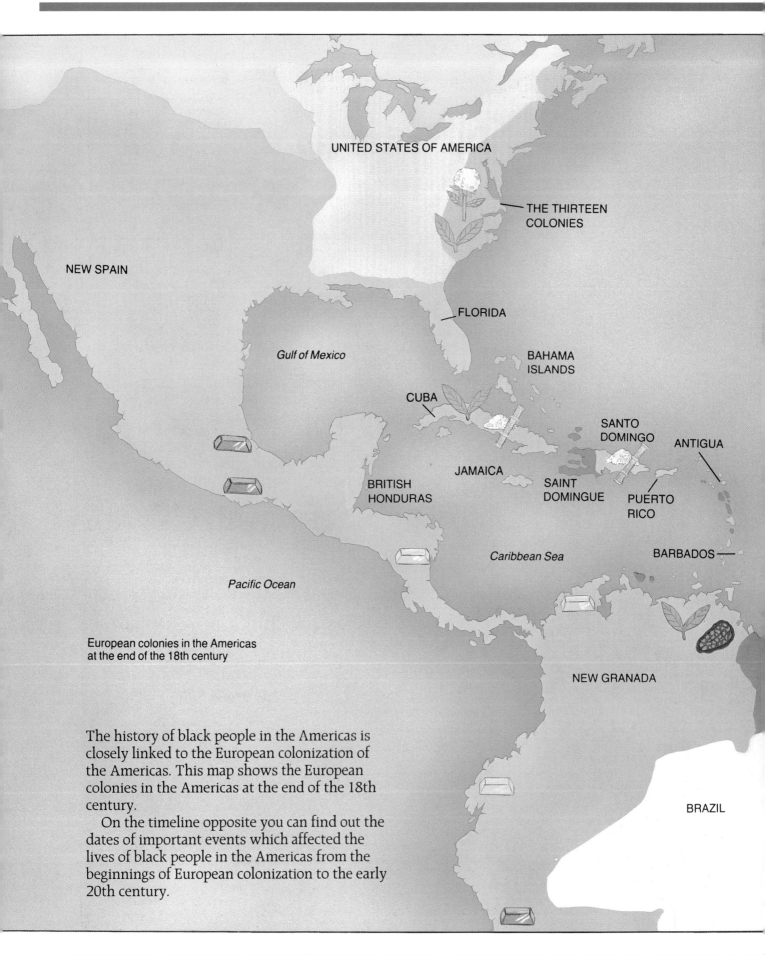

UNITED STATES OF AMERICA

THE THIRTEEN
COLONIES

NEW SPAIN

FLORIDA

Gulf of Mexico

BAHAMA
ISLANDS

CUBA

SANTO
DOMINGO

ANTIGUA

JAMAICA

SAINT
DOMINGUE

PUERTO
RICO

BRITISH
HONDURAS

Caribbean Sea

BARBADOS

Pacific Ocean

European colonies in the Americas
at the end of the 18th century

NEW GRANADA

BRAZIL

The history of black people in the Americas is
closely linked to the European colonization of
the Americas. This map shows the European
colonies in the Americas at the end of the 18th
century.

On the timeline opposite you can find out the
dates of important events which affected the
lives of black people in the Americas from the
beginnings of European colonization to the early
20th century.

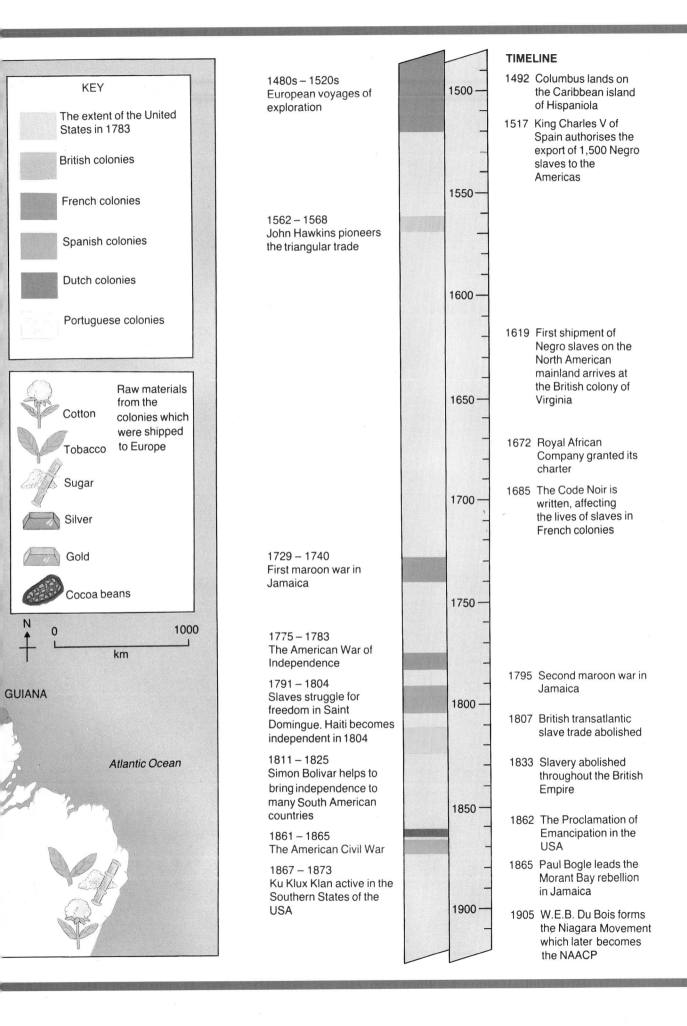

KEY

The extent of the United States in 1783

British colonies

French colonies

Spanish colonies

Dutch colonies

Portuguese colonies

Raw materials from the colonies which were shipped to Europe

Cotton

Tobacco

Sugar

Silver

Gold

Cocoa beans

N

0   1000
km

GUIANA

Atlantic Ocean

1480s – 1520s
European voyages of exploration

1562 – 1568
John Hawkins pioneers the triangular trade

1729 – 1740
First maroon war in Jamaica

1775 – 1783
The American War of Independence

1791 – 1804
Slaves struggle for freedom in Saint Domingue. Haiti becomes independent in 1804

1811 – 1825
Simon Bolivar helps to bring independence to many South American countries

1861 – 1865
The American Civil War

1867 – 1873
Ku Klux Klan active in the Southern States of the USA

1500

1550

1600

1650

1700

1750

1800

1850

1900

TIMELINE

1492 Columbus lands on the Caribbean island of Hispaniola

1517 King Charles V of Spain authorises the export of 1,500 Negro slaves to the Americas

1619 First shipment of Negro slaves on the North American mainland arrives at the British colony of Virginia

1672 Royal African Company granted its charter

1685 The Code Noir is written, affecting the lives of slaves in French colonies

1795 Second maroon war in Jamaica

1807 British transatlantic slave trade abolished

1833 Slavery abolished throughout the British Empire

1862 The Proclamation of Emancipation in the USA

1865 Paul Bogle leads the Morant Bay rebellion in Jamaica

1905 W.E.B. Du Bois forms the Niagara Movement which later becomes the NAACP

Arriving in the Americas

Exploration and encounter

AIMS

Christopher Columbus sailed to the Americas in 1492. He is remembered as the European who 'discovered' the NEW WORLD**. In this unit we will look at clues which suggest that black Africans travelled to the Americas long before Columbus made his journey.**

We will find out that Europeans were in regular contact with black people in the 15th century. We shall also look at the involvement of black people in the exploration and COLONIZATION **of the Americas.**

On the morning of the 3rd August 1492, Christopher Columbus set sail with three ships from the Spanish port of Palos. His plan was to find a western route from Europe to Asia. You can see the route which he took in Source 1. Before Columbus's voyage, the Portuguese were already exploring the eastern route to Asia. In 1486, King John II of Portugal sent his navigator, Bartholomew Diaz, to find a route by sailing round Africa. Diaz reached as far as the southern tip of Africa in 1487 but he was forced back by storms in the Indian Ocean. Two years later, a German map-maker named Henricus Martellus drew a new map of the world (see Source 2). Martellus copied maps from Ancient Greece, but he also used the detailed measurements which Diaz recorded on his voyage.

Like Martellus, Columbus believed that the world was round and that if he set out across the 'Oceanus Occidental' (which you can see marked on Source 2) he would reach Asia. So it is not surprising that when a member of his crew sighted land on the 12th October 1492, Columbus thought he had discovered an island off the eastern coast of China.

SOURCE 1

Voyages made by European explorers in the late 15th and early 16th centuries.

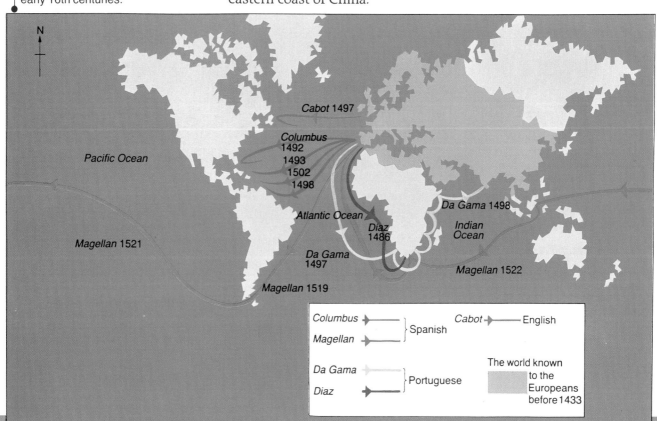

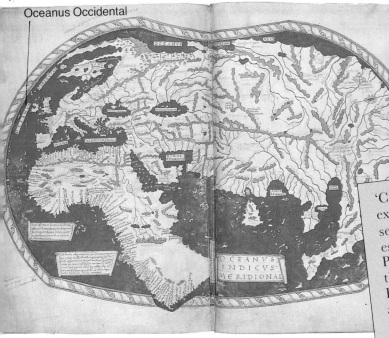

Oceanus Occidental

SOURCE 2

This map of the world was drawn by Henricus Martellus in 1489.

SOURCE 3

A modern historian describes European trading links with Africa in the 15th century.

'Columbus had, in 1481, commanded a ship in the expedition which the Portuguese government had sent to the Guinea coast. . . . The expedition was to establish trade, and every effort was made by the Portuguese to do so. They established contact with the Negro king and exchanged presents with him. Furthermore, they negotiated a treaty (worked out an agreement) which gave the Portuguese exclusive rights to exchange their goods for gold.'

Europe and the wider world

Columbus's voyage was by no means the first contact between white and non-white people. If you look at Source 2 again, you can see that the world known to the Europeans at the end of the 15th century included Africa and Asia. There were many contacts between Europeans and people from this wider world. Some of these contacts were for trading purposes: Columbus himself traded with West Africa in 1481 (see Source 3).

There was also contact through war. In 711 Spain was invaded by the MOORS from North Africa. Spain was then governed as part of the ISLAMIC EMPIRE. In the centuries that followed, Christians and Moors fought over Spanish territory and Moorish control weakened. The Moors finally surrendered their last stronghold at Granada in 1492. During this period, MUSLIMS of several different nationalities settled in Spain, see Source 4. The Moors introduced new styles of architecture and new crops such as SUGAR-CANE and rice. Many Arabic words were absorbed into the Spanish language.

After the Moors had been defeated there were still many black people living in Spain. There is evidence that members of Columbus's crew were from different ethnic backgrounds. In fact two of the ships in Columbus's expedition of 1492 were captained by the Pinzon brothers, who were known as the 'NEGRO Pinzons'.

SOURCE 4

This painting of a Moorish nobleman comes from the Alhambra Palace in Granada. It was built by the Moors in the 13th and 14th centuries.

1 What can you tell from Sources 1 and 3 about contacts between Europeans and black Africans at the end of the 15th century?

2 Look at Source 2 and compare it with a map of the world in a modern atlas. How accurate is the Martellus map?

Native Americans

Between 1492 and 1504, Columbus made four voyages to the islands of the Caribbean and parts of the South American mainland. He described the people he saw there as having copper-coloured skin and straight, black hair. Because Columbus believed that his voyages had taken him to Asia, he called the native people 'Indians'. Today historians have put forward four different ideas or theories to suggest how people may have settled in the Americas, see Sources 5 and 6.

Theory 1 The ancestors of the people seen by Columbus in the Americas may have come across a 'land-bridge' which linked north-eastern Asia with north-western America thousands of years ago. Today there is no land-bridge: the two continents are separated by the Bering Sea.

Theory 2 Settlers may have reached the Americas by 'island hopping' across the Pacific Ocean from south-eastern Asia.

Theory 3 The Vikings from present day Iceland, Norway and Sweden may have colonised the New World three centuries before Columbus arrived.

Theory 4 There is evidence that West Africans living in Mali and Guinea possessed the same level of technology as Europeans in the Middle Ages. Some historians have suggested that Africans may have reached the Americas before Columbus.

SOURCE 5
Theories which suggest how people might have arrived in the Americas.

SOURCE 6
This map shows the routes which people might have taken to reach the Americas.

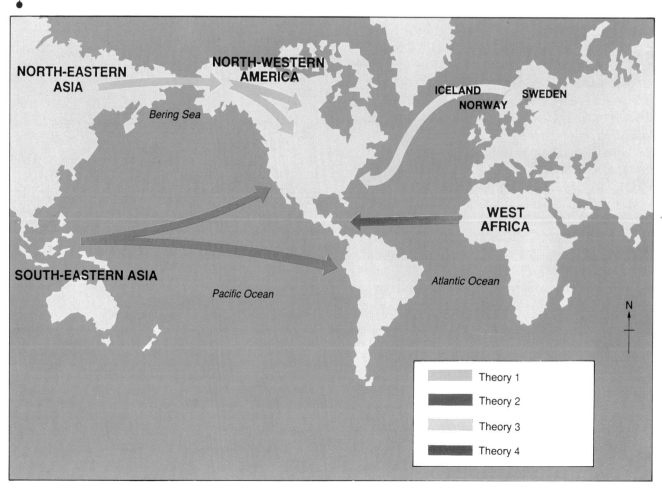

Theories and evidence

Theory 1 in Source 5 is the most widely accepted. However this theory claims that the people who settled in the Americas had no links with either Asia or Africa. On the other hand, Theory 4 suggests links between the Americas and Africa. If you look at the world map in a school atlas you will see that Europe is usually placed in the centre. If America is placed in the centre (as it is in Source 6) it is easier to understand that people from Asia or Africa may have reached the Americas either by accident or on a planned voyage.

Historians who support Theory 4 in Source 5 point to two expeditions organised by Emperor Abubakari of Mali in the early 14th century. Abubakari led the second expedition himself, see Source 7.

Historical clues

Historians sometimes work like detectives. Matching ARTEFACTS from two different places may suggest that people travelled between those places in the past. The giant rock carving, which you can see in Source 8, was found at La Venta in Mexico. The carved head has distinctive negroid features which make it similar to carvings found in West Africa. The head from La Venta gives support to the idea that people from Africa settled in the Americas.

Such detective work was also carried out at the time of Columbus's voyage. The spears described in Source 9 were sent by Columbus to royal ASSAYERS in Spain. They were found to be identical to spears discovered in West Africa by Portuguese merchants. From these findings it seemed that traders from the West African coast could have brought the spears to HISPANIOLA where they were found.

attainment target 2

1 Are the four theories in Source 5 facts or opinions? Explain your answer.

2 The movement of peoples described in each of the theories took place hundreds of years ago and we have very little evidence from that time. How has this affected the arguments?

3 Which facts seem to contradict Theory 3?

4 Which facts seem to support Theory 4?

5 Which of the four theories do you think is the more accurate? Explain your answer.

SOURCE 8
This carved head was found at La Venta in Mexico. It has been dated variously from the 1st to the 5th century BC.

In 1310, the Malian Emperor Abubakari II sent a fleet of 400 ships into the Atlantic Ocean towards America. Only one ship returned but could not report the fate of the others which seemed to have been swept away by the ocean currents. . . . In 1311 Abubakari . . . led another fleet of 400 ships across the Atlantic and never returned.

SOURCE 7
An account of Emperor Abubakari's expedition, written by a modern historian.

'While he was in Hispaniola for the second time the Indians told Columbus that there had come to (the island) black people who had the tops of their spears made of a metal which was 18 parts gold, six parts silver and eight parts copper.'

SOURCE 9
A description of the spears which Columbus sent to royal assayers in Spain, written by a modern historian.

SOURCE 10
The earliest known
portrait of native
South Americans.

African influences

Source 10 is the earliest known painting of
native South Americans. Like the Fulani woman
from West Africa, photographed in Source 11,
they are wearing solid gold nose and ear
ornaments and necklaces. The similarities in the
jewellery give strength to the idea that West
African influences were present in 16th century
South America. However it was slavery which
led to the enforced movement of African people
to the Americas on
a massive scale.

SOURCE 11
This photograph is of a woman from Mali, West Africa.
She is a member of the Fulani tribe.

The foundations of slavery

Slavery was not unknown in 15th century
Europe. There were Moorish slaves in Spain. The
Portuguese voyages along the West African coast
set up trading links for various items, including
slaves. However, it would be wrong to think that
slavery was introduced to Africa by Europeans.
In fact, African societies already practised
slavery. In Africa, slavery was used as a form of
punishment and wars were often fought for
slaves rather than territory. Slaves captured in
battle were sometimes sold to merchants who
would then sell them again at a profit.

With the arrival of the Portuguese and other
Europeans, African merchants began to ship
slaves to the coast to sell to their new customers.
The African slaves were then taken back to
Europe where they were sold at AUCTION. The
first European auction to include West African
slaves was held at Lagos in Portugal, in 1445.
You can read a description of this in Source 12.

'Those who had charge of the division of the
captives now arrived, and began to separate one
from another. They parted husbands from wives,
fathers from sons, brothers from brothers. No
respect was shown either to friends or relations. It
was a terrible scene of misery and disorder.'

SOURCE 12
A description of the Lagos slave
auction written by the
CHRONICLER, Azurara in 1445.

Slavery and Spanish exploration

When Columbus made his first voyage to the Americas in 1492, there were already black African slaves in Spain. In the timeline opposite you can see that some of these slaves were sent on the early Spanish voyages of exploration to the Americas. Black soldiers were also recruited by the Spanish CONQUISTADORS. Hernán Cortés (pictured in Source 13) invaded Mexico in 1519. There were black recruits in his army of 500 men.

SOURCE 13

Hernán Cortés invading Mexico, 1519.

1 Which events on the timeline show black people in important positions?

2 Which events on the timeline show the growth of slavery?

3 The decision taken in 1523 to limit the number of black people in the Americas did not last. Why were more black Africans taken to the Americas in spite of Spanish fears?

Black people and the colonization of the Americas.

1492 The 'Negro Pinzons' captained one of the ships on Columbus's first voyage to the Americas.

The Spanish began sending African slaves, bought from the Portuguese, to the Caribbean.

Thirty Negroes helped the explorer Balboa to hack his way through the tropical undergrowth to reach the Pacific Ocean.

1505 The Spanish signed a contract for a regular supply of Africans as slaves. Spanish merchants made arrangements with the Portuguese to guarantee this supply.

1513

1517 Hernán Cortés, from Spain, invaded Mexico. One of the Negroes in his army of 500 men found some wheat grains in his ration of rice. He planted them and so was the first person to introduce wheat to the North American mainland.

1519

1523 There were so many Negroes in Mexico that the Spanish colonists decided to limit their number because they were afraid of a revolt.

The king of Spain sent soldiers to the island of Puerto Rico to fight the native people. The Spanish colonists believed that Negro slaves had caused the troubles on the island. The king was therefore asked not to send any more slaves.

1532

1540 Church records show that a Negro in Quivira, Mexico, became a priest.

Slaves from Africa

Throughout the 16th century Spain and Portugal dominated the colonization of the Americas. This required much exhausting physical work: clearing woodland, planting, cultivating and processing new crops, mining and building. The Spanish and Portuguese were reluctant to do this work themselves. They had gone to the New World to live like gentlemen. They preferred to use the native people of the Americas to provide slave labour (see Source 14). These people were forced to work under harsh conditions. They were also exposed to new and fatal diseases such as smallpox and measles, carried over by the Europeans.

Roots of American slavery

Many of the native people died, so the Spanish and Portuguese turned to West Africa to supply them with slaves (see Source 15). The Portuguese trading posts along the West African coast became the grim places where slaves were inspected, branded and imprisoned before being shipped to the Americas. In Source 16 you can see a modern photograph of one of these forts. Source 17 is a description of how slaves were treated by European merchants in West Africa.

SOURCE 14
Spanish colonists forcing the native population to work in the Americas.

'Bartolomé de las Casas, a Dominican priest . . . travelled to Spain to plead for the abolition of native slavery. . . . Las Casas, haunted at the prospect of seeing before his eyes the total destruction of a population within one generation, hit on the solution of importing the more robust Negroes from Africa; in 1517, Charles V (of Spain) authorised the export of 1500 slaves to San Domingo, and thus priest and king launched on the world the American slave trade and slavery.'

SOURCE 15
A modern historian, C.L.R. James, explains how the beginnings of African slavery can be traced to the actions of Charles V of Spain and Bartolomé de las Casas.

'As the slaves come down to Fida from the inland country, they are put into a booth or prison . . . near the beach. When the Europeans are to receive them, they are brought out onto a large plain, where the ship's surgeons examine every part of everyone of them. . . . Those who are declared good and sound are . . . marked on the breast with a red-hot iron, imprinting the mark of the French, English or Dutch companies. . . . The branded slaves after this are returned to their former booths where they await shipment, sometimes 10-15 days.'

SOURCE 17
This description was written by John Barbat who travelled to Africa in the 18th century.

SOURCE 16
Elmina Fort, built in Ghana by the Portuguese in 1482.

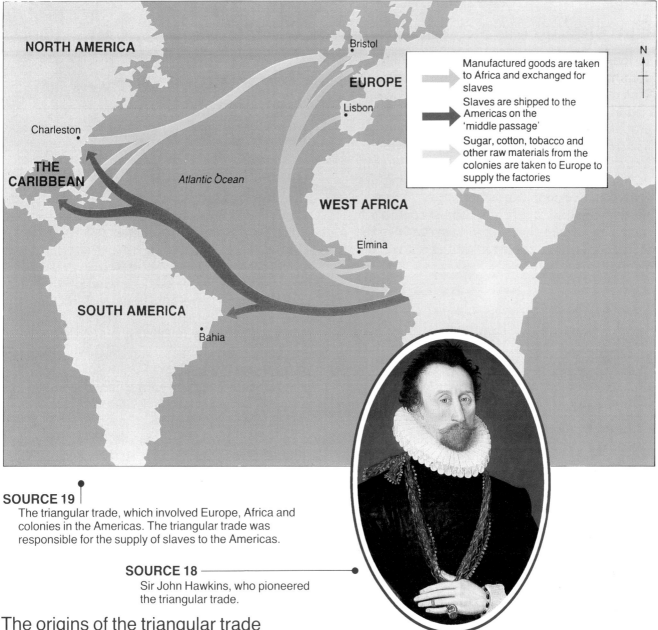

SOURCE 19
The triangular trade, which involved Europe, Africa and colonies in the Americas. The triangular trade was responsible for the supply of slaves to the Americas.

SOURCE 18
Sir John Hawkins, who pioneered the triangular trade.

Map legend:
Manufactured goods are taken to Africa and exchanged for slaves
Slaves are shipped to the Americas on the 'middle passage'
Sugar, cotton, tobacco and other raw materials from the colonies are taken to Europe to supply the factories

Map labels: NORTH AMERICA, EUROPE, Bristol, Lisbon, Charleston, THE CARIBBEAN, Atlantic Ocean, WEST AFRICA, Elmina, SOUTH AMERICA, Bahia, N

The origins of the triangular trade

In 1562 an Englishman named John Hawkins (pictured in Source 18) organised a trading voyage to the Spanish colonies. His ship carried cloth and other goods from England, as well as slaves which he had bought on the West African coast. He traded with Spanish merchants in the Caribbean. He exchanged his goods and slaves for a cargo of sugar, leather and silver, which he took back to England. Hawkins wanted to break the Spanish and Portuguese control of trade in the Caribbean. He made three more voyages between 1562 and 1568, but he failed to open up the Caribbean to British merchants. However, his ventures were important because they established a new pattern of trade – the triangular trade (see Source 19).

ACTIVITY

Get into groups of three or four for this activity.

What seems to be at the root of the slave trade with the Americas?

- laziness: the Spanish colonists preferred not to work themselves
- greed: there were big profits to be made from trade with the Americas
- racism: Europeans regarded Africans and native Americans as inferior people.

Use what you have read so far in this book to support your decision.

Europe and the slave trade

In the early 17th century, other European countries began to challenge Spanish and Portuguese control of the Americas. The French and British sailed along the North American coastline and established their own colonies. The first permanent British settlement was founded at Jamestown in the colony of Virginia in 1607. The early colonists began planting tobacco for export. The tobacco PLANTATIONS needed a steady supply of labour. European merchants began shipping African slaves to the North American colonies as well as to the Caribbean, see Source 20.

> About the last of August came in a Dutch Man of Warre (ship) that sold us twenty Negars (Negroes).

SOURCE 20
John Rolfe, an English colonist, reports on the first shipment of slaves to Virginia in 1619.

SOURCE 22
The guinea was struck in 1663 to commemorate the founding of The Royal Adventurers which was renamed as the Royal African Company in 1672. The coin was originally made of gold from Guinea in West Africa.

'Ten spotted sashes per slave.
Three pieces flowered silk per slave.
Four pieces flowered linen per slave.
Twelve gallons of brandy per slave.
Three cases of English spirits per slave.'

SOURCE 21
A price list for the exchange of slaves used at the West African port of Arda in 1680.

The middle passage

The growing European colonies in the Americas all relied upon the profitable triangular trade which John Hawkins had pioneered. Products from the New World colonies such as tobacco, coffee, rum, sugar and cotton were in great demand in Europe. Goods from Europe were sold in Africa in exchange for slaves. In Source 21 you can read part of a price list used by a slave merchant working for the Royal African Company. This company started trading with Africa in 1663 (see Source 22). In 1672 it was granted its CHARTER by King Charles II and it dominated the British slave trade until the middle of the 18th century. Once the slaves had been bought by European merchants, they were shipped across the Atlantic on the so-called middle passage; (look back at Source 19).

Conditions on board the slave ships were appalling. The European merchants wanted to make a large profit, so the ships were filled with as many slaves as possible, see Sources 23 and 24. Sometimes the height between decks was only 50 centimetres. Slaves were chained together so that they could not move or even turn over. Diseases spread quickly in these conditions. Sometimes as many as a quarter of the slaves on board died before they reached the Americas.

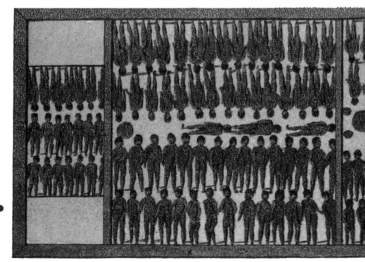

SOURCE 23
A plan of a slave ship. The Portuguese called their slave ships *tumbeiros*, which means coffins.

'God be praised the *Hannah* under the command of Thomas Godfrey . . . arrived at Barbados on the 18th of June with 417 Negroes not losing more than 13, they came in good condition but the factors (merchants) complain of the number of women to be extraordinary (very high) which will much impair the sales (lower the price).'

SOURCE 25

Part of a letter from the headquarters of the Royal African Company to one of its merchants based at a port on the West African coast. It was written in 1688.

SOURCE 24

This painting of slaves huddled below deck on a Spanish slave ship bound for the Caribbean was made by a British naval officer in 1818.

Slave auctions

For the slave merchants, a large number of deaths on the middle passage would mean a loss of profit. Merchants were not interested in the slaves' welfare, only the prices that they would fetch when they were sold, see Source 25. You can see a picture of a slave auction in Source 26. No respect was shown for the slaves at auction: they were paraded, sometimes naked, in front of prospective buyers who were allowed to examine them for physical defects. Once a sale had been agreed, the new owners would have the slaves branded as their property.

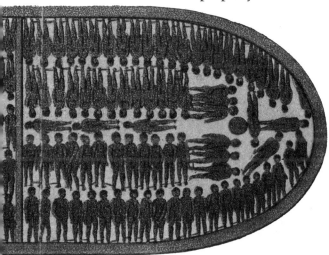

SOURCE 26

A 19th century painting of a slave auction.

attainment target 1

1 Look at the timeline on page 11 and at Source 20, written in 1619. What differences were there between the position of the black people who accompanied Columbus and Balboa and those described in Source 20?

2 Look at Sources 16 to 26. Choose **four** which you think show four different sides of the slave trade. Explain your choice.

3 Choose three sources from Sources 20, 21, 23, 25 and 26 and explain what evidence they give us about white attitudes to slavery.

4 Are the same attitudes to be found in all these sources? Explain your answer.

Slavery

The Church and slavery

AIMS

In this unit we shall look first at the attitude of the Church to slavery. We shall then look at the working conditions of slaves on the plantations. We shall see how slaves were treated by their owners and by the laws of the European colonies. The unit ends by looking at the life that the slaves made for themselves.

For many centuries before Columbus's voyages and in the centuries that followed, the Church had a powerful influence on government. Sometimes bishops, archbishops and cardinals held important positions in government. Cardinal Ximenes, who is pictured in Source 1, was an influential Spanish church leader. In 1502, he was authorised by Queen Isabella to issue a decree that all Moors living in Spain should either be converted to Christianity or forced to leave the country. Converting 'non-believers' to the Christian faith was a principal aim of the Church. This aim also influenced the attitude of the Church towards slavery.

MISSIONARIES who went to the Americas during the early years of colonization tried to protect the native American population. You can see a photograph of one of the early missions in Source 2. As a result, royal advisers in Spain drew up a list of regulations, known as the Laws of Burgos. These laws set out basic rights for the native American people: they should not be forced into slavery and they should be converted to Christianity by peaceful means.

SOURCE 1

This wood carving from Granada cathedral shows Cardinal Ximenes with King Ferdinand and Queen Isabella of Spain. They are shown riding into Granada after the city was surrendered by the Moors in 1492.

SOURCE 2

An early mission built by the Spanish in New Mexico in the 16th century.

16

Native Americans or Negroes?

However it was difficult to enforce these laws or to control the behaviour of the Spanish colonists. Whatever they had been in Spain, the colonists wanted to be gentlemen in the Americas. They were not willing to work in the hot sun, in the alligator and snake-infested swamps. They wanted cheap slaves.

Although the Church did make efforts to protect the native Americans, it did not want to outlaw slavery completely. The Church had become very wealthy from the profits of the plantations which relied on cheap slave labour (Source 3). So although the Church worked to release the native American people from slavery, it did not condemn the introduction of African slaves to the Americas. In Source 4 you can read part of a letter written by Judge Zuazo on the island of Hispaniola, recommending that Africans should be imported as slaves. He went on to suggest that whipping or cutting off their ears would make them obedient. Bartolomé de las Casas (a Spanish priest who is pictured in Source 5) also argued that Negro slavery was preferable to native American slavery.

SOURCE 3

Profits from the plantations in the American colonies contributed to the wealth of the Church in Spain. Many fine cathedrals and churches were built or enlarged during the 16th century.

'There is urgent need for Negro slaves. Let ships bring many male and female Negroes between the ages of 15 and 20 years. They will be made to adopt our customs and they will be settled in villages and married to their women folk. The burden of work of the Indians will be eased.'

SOURCE 4

A letter from Judge Zuazo of Hispaniola to Cardinal Ximenes, written in 1518. He is asking for more slaves to be sent to the island.

SOURCE 5

Bartolomé de las Casas (1474-1566). He supported bringing African slaves to the Americas.

1 What evidence do we have about the attitude of the Christian Church to black slavery?

2 Cardinal Ximenes has asked you to reply to the letter from Judge Zuazo of Hispaniola (Source 4). Write a letter either granting or refusing his request.

Sugar plantations

Sugar became increasingly popular in Europe in the 17th century (see Source 6). The Spanish were the first to grow sugar-cane in the Caribbean. By the 17th century other European countries were also producing it in their colonies.

Sugar production rose steadily to meet the new demand (Source 7). More slaves were shipped from Africa to the Caribbean to work on the plantations. The plantation system became completely dependent on slave labour, as one 18th century plantation owner comments in Source 8. For example in 1645 there were reported to be 5,680 African slaves on the island of Barbados, by 1667 the number had risen to 82,023.

Slave labour

Growing and harvesting the cane and then extracting the sugar from it needed a lot of labour. When sugar-cane is cut it quickly loses its sweetness and so the plantation workers had to process the cane immediately. The slaves worked for long hours under unpleasant and sometimes dangerous conditions to extract the sugar from the cane.

Each plantation had its own windmill which drove the heavy iron rollers for crushing the cane. There would also be a boiling house and out-buildings where the sugary liquid was cooled and dried. A survey made in Barbados in 1683 recorded 358 sugar works on the island. Some of the windmills can still be seen in Barbados today (see Source 9). You can see slaves working in a boiling house in Source 10.

> 'Negroes are the sinews of a plantation and it is as impossible for a man to make sugar without the assistance of Negroes, as to make bricks without straw.'

SOURCE 8
John Pinney, who owned plantations on the island of Nevis in the Caribbean, made this comment in 1764.

> Sugar has now succeeded honey . . . yet being much used produces dangerous effects in the body: too much use of it . . . rots the teeth, making them look black.

SOURCE 6
A comment on the popularity of sugar, written by James Hart, a doctor, in 1633.

Colonies	Production (Yearly average in tonnes)	
	1741-1745	1766-1770
British	41,702	81,573
French	65,713	79,173
Dutch	9,358	10,288
Spanish	2,032	10,160
Danish	742	8,362
Total	119,547	189,556

SOURCE 7
A table to show sugar production in the Caribbean between 1741 and 1770.

SOURCE 9
A sugar-mill in Barbados.

SOURCE 10
Slaves working in the boiling house on a plantation sugar factory. This watercolour was painted by W. Clark in 1823 when he visited the island of Antigua.

'Their buildings are very fair and beautiful and their houses are like castles.'

SOURCE 11
A description of plantation houses in Barbados.

SOURCE 12
Sunbury plantation house, Barbados.

Masters and merchants

Plantation owners became very wealthy and as one 17th century visitor to Barbados commented, they lived in fine mansions (see Source 11). Some of these plantation houses, like the one in Source 12, have been restored and are open to the public as museums.

European ports made huge profits from the triangular trade and the Caribbean sugar plantations. London was the most important slave trading centre in Britain until the Royal African Company's monopoly of the trade ended in 1698. After this date, Bristol and Liverpool rapidly developed as important slaving centres, see Source 13.

In Bristol alone, sugar imports almost doubled in the first half of the 18th century. The merchants often invested their profits in local industries which manufactured goods for export to Africa.

SOURCE 13
Part of Bristol harbour, painted around 1750.

SOURCE 14
This improved model of Whitney's cotton gin was used in the 19th century.

Cotton plantations

While the prosperity of the Caribbean rested on sugar, in the Southern States of America, cotton was the main source of wealth. The cotton plantations grew in both size and number throughout the 18th century and demanded a large slave workforce.

In 1793, Eli Whitney invented a machine called the cotton gin, see Source 14. The cotton gin was used for separating the cotton fibres from the seeds. Slaves operating the gin could separate fifty times more cotton per day than they could by hand. This huge increase in production set off an economic revolution in the Southern States. It was helped by an increasing demand for cotton from the Northern States and Great Britain.

SOURCE 15
Cromford cotton mill in Derbyshire which was built by Richard Arkwright, a leading 18th century industrialist.

> **attainment target 2**
>
> **A** Picking the cotton was pleasant, easy work. Slaves worked at a slow pace, taking their families out to the fields to enjoy the open air.
>
> **B** Picking the cotton was hard, boring, gruelling work. Slave-owners expected all their slaves and their families to help.
>
> **1** Are statements **A** and **B** fact, opinion, or partly fact and partly opinion? Explain your answer.
>
> **2** How far do Sources 16 and 17 support either statement **A** or statement **B**?
>
> **3** From what you have read so far in this book, which statement do you think is more truthful? Explain your choice.
>
> **4** What other sources in this book would you use to support your answer to question **3**?

Exporting cotton

For most of the 18th century, cotton manufacture in Great Britain was a cottage industry: men and women did the spinning and weaving by hand in their homes. At the end of the 18th century new inventions meant that spinning and weaving was done in factories on a much larger scale, see Source 15. Cotton exports from the southern plantations increased rapidly to meet this demand. In just two years between 1792 and 1794, exports rose from 62,596 kilograms to 726,208 kilograms.

Contrasting lifestyles

By 1860, slaves accounted for more than one third of the population in the Southern States. The success of the cotton economy and the gracious lifestyles of the plantation owners depended on the relentless toil of the slaves. The planters enjoyed many entertainments: they held splendid balls in the grounds of their fine mansions and gambled at their private race tracks. Slaves were often taken to race meetings and used as payment for last-minute bets placed by their owners.

Slaves cultivating the cotton worked long hours, even in the sweltering summer heat. The work was particularly hard at harvest-time. The cotton BOLLS ripened unevenly, so the same field would have to be picked at least three times. Source 16 shows a slave family on a cotton plantation and you can see slaves picking cotton in Source 17. Planters needed about 100 slaves for every 2,500 hectares. If a harvest was good and the crop had not been damaged by frost, planters could expect to make a profit of $250 per year on the cost of keeping each slave.

SOURCE 16
An early 19th century photograph showing a slave family with baskets of cotton bolls on a plantation in Georgia.

SOURCE 17
This 19th century print shows slaves picking cotton at harvest-time.

Slaves and racism

As Europeans prospered on the colonial trade, so they tried to justify slavery. They did so on racist grounds. Africans were said to be racially inferior, with no understanding of freedom. They did not deserve, or need, human rights or dignity. Everything African was dismissed: even the slaves' African names were not to be used. They were given European Christian names. On leaving West Africa, families were broken up. Husbands, wives and children could be sent to plantations in different parts of America or on islands hundreds of miles apart. The law, often influenced by the Church, supported this denial of human rights.

> The slaves live in small, oblong thatched huts, in which they have all their moveables or goods, which are generally a mat to lie on, a pot of earth to boil their victuals (food) in . . . and a calabash (container made from a pumpkin shell) or two for cups and spoons.

SOURCE 18
A description of slave huts in Jamaica, written by Sir Hans Sloane when he visited the island in 1687.

> 'Now for the Negroes . . . the 50 men shall be allowed yearly but three pairs of canvas drawers (underwear) a piece which at two SHILLINGS a pair is six shillings . . . The women shall be allowed but two petticoats a piece yearly, at four shillings a piece, which is eight shillings yearly. So the yearly charge of the 50 men Negroes is 15 pounds and of the women it is 20 pounds.'

SOURCE 20
In this extract from *A true and exact history of the island of Barbados* written by Richard Ligon in 1657, the costs of clothing slaves on a plantation are recorded.

Living and working conditions

The lives of black slaves working on the plantations in the Caribbean and in the North American colonies were totally regulated by their white owners. Slaves had no control over the length of their working day or the conditions in which they lived. Often their living quarters were cramped and poorly equipped, see Sources 18 and 19. Even the slaves' food and clothing were rationed by the plantation owners, as Source 20 reveals.

SOURCE 19
A 19th century photograph of one of the last slave huts in Barbados.

The slave codes

In addition to the rules laid down by plantation owners, there were basic codes of law which outlined how slaves should behave and be treated. All the French colonies of the Caribbean used a set of laws known as the *Code Noir*, written in 1685. All slaves had to be baptised into the Christian faith and were forbidden to worship the gods of their forefathers. They could not speak their own languages or keep their customs and traditions.

Under the *Code Noir* slaves could not carry weapons or gather together in groups. They were not allowed to own property. If they grew crops on the small pieces of land around their huts, they were forbidden to sell any of the produce. The *Code Noir* also listed punishments for slaves breaking its laws (see Source 21). If slaves were caught attempting to escape, they would be branded using irons like those in Source 22. Owners were even given the right to kill a slave who had tried to run away several times.

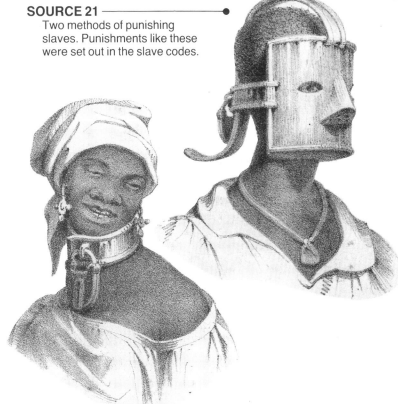

SOURCE 21

Two methods of punishing slaves. Punishments like these were set out in the slave codes.

---

1 Why do we have to rely on white sources for most of the information in this unit?

2 What was the attitude of slave owners to the family life of the slaves?

3 Do you think slaves were better off in French or British colonies?

SOURCE 22

Branding irons were used to identify slaves or as a form of punishment.

Slaves in the British colonies

The British colonies did not have a set of rules like the *Code Noir*. At first slavery was just accepted without any legal basis. Laws were made later by the colonists, who were often the plantation owners themselves. In most British colonies, slaves were given the legal status of CHATTELS: they were regarded as property which could be bought or sold. They had no basic human rights. As the Church was not involved in making British slave laws, plantation owners in the British colonies were not expected to convert their slaves to Christianity.

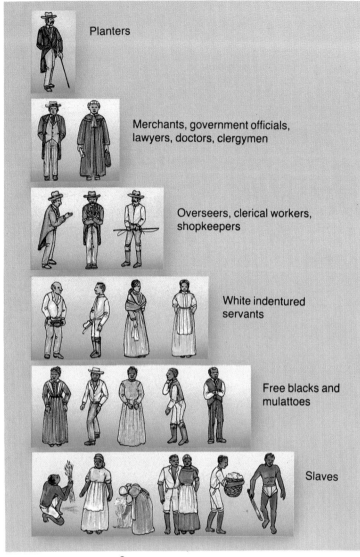

Planters

Merchants, government officials, lawyers, doctors, clergymen

Overseers, clerical workers, shopkeepers

White indentured servants

Free blacks and mulattoes

Slaves

SOURCE 24
The social pyramid found in American colonies during slavery.

Plantation society

The racist treatment of slaves by the law can also be seen in the position of slaves in society. Richard Ligon, who visited Barbados in 1657, described three broad social divisions, see Source 23. Source 24 gives a more detailed breakdown of plantation society.

White people in society

At the top of the social pyramid were the wealthy planters and their families. They usually owned about 40 slaves in domestic service as well as many more who worked on the plantations. Many planters retired to Europe when they had made their fortunes, leaving their plantations in the hands of agents. John Pinney, who is pictured in Source 25, was one of these absentee landlords. He owned sugar plantations in Nevis. Absentee landlords living in Britain were often able to influence Parliament to support the slave trade.

White merchants, government officials, lawyers, doctors and clergymen also ranked highly in plantation societies. Less wealthy members of the white society included OVERSEERS, clerical workers and shopkeepers. Next came poor whites, some of whom had been indentured servants. Indentured servants were people who were taken from Europe to work for plantation owners. They had to work as slaves for up to seven years before they were granted their freedom and a small plot of land.

SOURCE 23
Another extract from *A true and exact history of the island of Barbados*.

'The island is divided into three sorts of men: masters, servants and slaves.'

SOURCE 25
This portrait of John Pinney (1740-1818) was painted around 1793.

Free black people

Not all black people were owned as slaves. Children of free European fathers and slave mothers were called MULATTOES. Some of them were allowed an education and got respectable jobs as clerical workers or craftspeople. Occasionally, black slaves were granted freedom by their owners in return for many years of faithful service. Others ran away from the plantations and set up outlawed communities in remote places.

Slaves

However the vast majority of black people were slaves for life, see Source 26. Household slaves (like the black maid in Source 27), and those who were employed as skilled manual workers, usually received the best treatment. Then there were slaves who were given positions of responsibility to make sure that orders from the overseers were carried out.

Field hands and slaves working in the plantation factories were the lowest in rank and had the worst living conditions. Planters discriminated between slaves who had been born in the colonies, known as creoles, and those shipped from Africa. They believed that creoles were better workers because they were 'seasoned' and used to the plantation routine.

SOURCE 26

A photograph from 1857 showing slaves standing in order of their rank on a United States plantation.

SOURCE 27

This painting from around 1790 shows a black maid looking after her master's two young sons.

Slave culture

Slaves were excluded from the world of their owners. They were denied the rights which their owners took for granted and were trapped by their colour and status at the bottom of the social pyramid. Cut off from white society in so many ways, they created their own communities based on their own cultural traditions and religious beliefs.

The legal codes of some colonies stated that the slaves should be baptised into the Christian faith. However colonists did not give their slaves any religious teaching or bring them to church. The only Christian values which the slaves were taught were those emphasising their duty to be obedient and faithful. However, for the slaves themselves, the Christian faith brought comfort and relief. Equality on earth was impossible, but Christianity promised complete equality after death, in the Kingdom of Heaven.

SOURCE 29
Slaves in the Caribbean used African voodoo rituals in their worship. Voodoo ceremonies, like this one from Haiti, are still performed in the Caribbean today.

SOURCE 28
This is a modern photograph of a traditional funeral ceremony in Mali, West Africa. Slaves who were taken to the Americas kept many of their African customs alive.

1 How do you think slaves were able to keep their beliefs and customs alive?
2 How do you think slaves were able to keep their music alive?
3 What did Christianity seem to offer the slaves?

Forms of worship

Black slaves were not allowed to worship with their white masters, so they held their own religious meetings, often in secret. These meetings combined Christian elements with customs from Africa, see Sources 28 and 29. Leaders of African cults like VOODOO and OBEAH were powerful people in the slave communities and often became church elders. Some forms of Christianity which were fused with African beliefs, such as Pocomania, still survive in the Caribbean today.

African traditions also survived in the music and songs of the slaves. In Source 30 you can see slaves dancing to the music and rhythms of African instruments. The emotional style of black churches today has roots which have survived the brutality of the slave plantations. Even the spirituals which the slaves sang in their religious meetings had origins in African music. You can read the words from a popular spiritual hymn in Source 31.

SOURCE 30
This 18th century painting shows slaves playing African instruments and dancing on a plantation in South Carolina.

Steal away, steal away, steal away to Jesus,
Steal away, steal away home.
I ain't got long to stay here,
My Lord he calls me,
He calls me by the thunder,
The trumpet sounds within a'ma soul,
I ain't got long to stay here.
Steal away, steal away, steal away to Jesus,
Steal away, steal away home.
Green trees a'bending,
Poor sinner standing a'trembling,
The trumpet sounds within a'ma soul,
I ain't got long to stay here.

SOURCE 31
A spiritual hymn.

Slave resistance

Protests and punishments

The men and women usually remembered for fighting to bring slavery to an end are the white ABOLITIONISTS. However the slaves themselves were the first to struggle against slavery, making great sacrifices.

There were revolts on board slave ships. Many Africans threw themselves overboard, believing that death would return them to their home country, see Source 1. Protests took place on the plantations. Slaves refused to work or deliberately injured themselves so that they would be unable to carry out their duties. Female slaves even aborted their unborn children rather than bring them into a world of cruelty and hardship.

Individuals who protested in these ways were severely punished or even killed as a warning to the other slaves, see Source 2. Crucifixion, burning and starvation were all legal penalties which could be used by the white planters against their slaves. As the slave population grew, organised rebellions involving large numbers of slaves became more frequent. The slave owners found these uprisings more difficult to put down. In South Carolina, white planters witnessed a number of slave revolts. In 1734 they wrote to the British government, outlining their fears. You can read part of this letter in Source 3.

SOURCE 1
This dramatic painting by Turner captures the horrors of the middle passage. Many slaves committed suicide by drowning themselves.

SOURCE 2
Jamaican slaves being punished in a 'house of correction'. Some are being forced to drive a treadmill, others are in chains or are being whipped.

Revolts

A Jamaican slave called Tacky led that island's most serious slave rebellion, in 1769. The rebels broke into a store to get weapons and attacked many estates. Over 400 slaves and 60 whites were killed.

On February 23rd 1763, there was a slave revolt in what is now Guyana, but was then the Dutch colony of Berbice. The leader was called Kofi, and the rebels were able to defy the authorities for nine months. Today, February 23rd is a day of celebration in Guyana.

In the United States the largest and bloodiest slave revolt was mounted by Nat Turner and his followers in 1831 in Virginia. Turner led about 80 slaves during the revolt which lasted for only 48 hours. They killed 55 whites. Sixteen of the rebels were executed after the revolt and Turner himself was captured two months later and hanged.

'We are subject to many dangers from the great number of Negroes that are now among us, who amount at least to twenty-two thousand persons, and are three to one of all your Majesty's white subjects in this province (region). Insurrections (riots) against us have often been attempted.'

SOURCE 3
A letter from the colonists in South Carolina to the British government, written in 1734.

SOURCE 4
This 19th century painting shows a fugitive slave family escaping to the North on a stolen horse.

Running away

The only option left for many slaves was to try to escape. In the United States, slaves fled from plantations in the South to the Northern States and Canada where there was no slavery. The journey to freedom, which became known as the Underground Railroad (Source 4) was difficult and dangerous. Harriet Tubman escaped on the Underground Railroad from a Maryland cotton plantation in 1849. She then made 19 trips back to the Southern States and helped hundreds of slaves to freedom. In 1850, the government passed the Fugitive Slave Act. This meant that people in the free Northern States could be forced to return runaway slaves to their owners in the South, see Source 5. Plantation owners hired spies and hunters to recapture missing slaves.

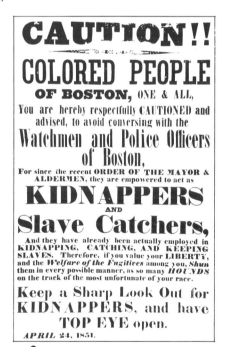

CAUTION!!
COLORED PEOPLE
OF BOSTON, ONE & ALL,
You are hereby respectfully CAUTIONED and advised, to avoid conversing with the
Watchmen and Police Officers of Boston,
For since the recent ORDER OF THE MAYOR & ALDERMEN, they are empowered to act as
KIDNAPPERS
AND
Slave Catchers,
And they have already been actually employed in KIDNAPPING, CATCHING, AND KEEPING SLAVES. Therefore, if you value your LIBERTY, and the *Welfare of the Fugitives* among you, *Shun* them in every possible manner, as so many *HOUNDS* on the track of the most unfortunate of your race.
Keep a Sharp Look Out for KIDNAPPERS, and have TOP EYE open.
APRIL 24, 1851.

SOURCE 5
This placard was issued to warn fugitive slaves about the dangers of being recaptured.

---

1 What different kinds of resistance to slavery are described here?

2 There were still slave rebellions despite previous punishments. What does this tell us about the lives of the slaves?

3 Tacky, Kofi and Nat Turner were treated as criminals at the time of their revolts. Now they are regarded as heroes. Why is this?

The Jamaican maroons

When the British captured Jamaica from Spain in 1655, some of the slaves escaped. They went into the thickly-wooded mountains of the island (Source 6) and set up free black communities. They were known as MAROONS. African culture flourished within the maroon communities. After Jamaica became one of the British colonies of the Caribbean, the first reported slave rebellion took place in 1673 when 200 slaves escaped from a single plantation and joined the maroons. More and more slaves fled their plantations to live in the maroon towns, see Source 7. In Source 8 you can read how one white planter from Jamaica described the situation.

The maroons often raided the slave plantations, setting fire to the cane-fields and outhouses, killing animals and carrying away the slaves. Source 9 shows a maroon ambush on a plantation. The maroons knew the terrain of the country and so they were able to make surprise attacks and evade capture.

SOURCE 6
In the 17th and 18th centuries, many slaves escaped to the mountainous countryside of Jamaica.

SOURCE 7
An 18th century drawing of Trelawny, a maroon town in Jamaica.

SOURCE 8
A comment on the situation in Jamaica, written by a planter in 1733.

No man . . . can be said to be master of a slave. Many of them are not doing half their work that they used to do, nor dare their master punish them, for the least disgust will probably cause them to make their escape and join the rebels.

The maroon wars

Two wars were fought between the maroons and the British colonists: the first started in about 1729 and lasted for over ten years, the second broke out in 1795 and lasted for six months.

The maroons were led by a man named Cudjoe during the first war. Under Cudjoe's skilful leadership, they defended themselves successfully against the British authorities. The planters and their government were faced with a dilemma: if they fought on to wipe out the maroon communities, they might cause a general uprising among the slaves. So the colonists signed a treaty with the maroon leaders, see Source 10. The treaty allowed the maroons to remain in their free communities on conditions: some of them could be used as a kind of police force to prevent any further planned escapes of slaves from the plantations.

The second maroon war

Although it became more difficult for slaves to rebel after the first maroon war, revolts continued to take place. After a shaky peace interrupted by several bloody disturbances, a second maroon war broke out in 1795. During this second conflict, more slaves joined the maroons. Once again they were able to defend themselves against the authorities. The fighting ended when a second peace treaty was drawn up between the British and the maroons.

ACTIVITY

Get into groups of four. You are all slaves on a plantation in Jamaica in the 18th century. Your master is particularly brutal. What can you do?

- one is for running away to join the maroons, who are poor but free
- one is for finding the chance to kill your master
- one is for keeping quiet
- one puts his or her trust in the Christian belief in a better life after death

Discuss your points of view.

Slave revolts in Saint Domingue

At the end of the 18th century, the French colony of Saint Domingue, which is shown in Source 11, was the richest colony in the New World. It supplied the world with sugar, cocoa, coffee, spices and precious wood. Ships from many different countries visited and traded with the colony. Its main cities of Port-au-Prince and Cap Français were flourishing trading ports, as Source 12 shows.

Class structure

Like other plantation societies, Saint Domingue had a divided class structure. The most powerful members of society were the white planters and the royal officials from France who governed the colony. They were known as the *grands blancs*. Then came the less wealthy whites or *petits blancs* who worked as craftspeople or overseers. Below the white classes were the mulattoes and free Negroes. Although they owned land and property, they were denied social and political equality with the whites. Finally came the slaves imported from Africa who numbered over 450,000 by 1789.

SOURCE 11

The French colony of Saint Domingue, in the Caribbean.

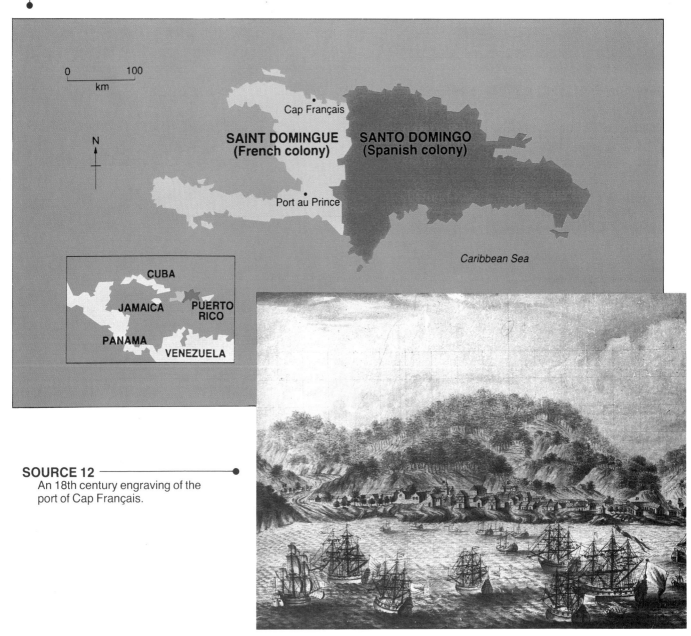

SOURCE 12

An 18th century engraving of the port of Cap Français.

SOURCE 13
A placard from the French Revolution. It is calling for a new republic founded upon liberty, equality and fraternity.

The French Revolution

The impact of the French Revolution of 1789 on such a society was enormous. In France the revolution gave power to a National Assembly and limited the power of the monarch (Source 13). The new revolutionary leaders made a declaration of rights for all free people living in France or its colonies. They also abolished the feudal system and the privileges which the wealthy landowners had enjoyed.

The Revolution and Saint Domingue

Where did that leave the slave-owners of Saint Domingue? For their part, the mulattoes were given new hopes for equality as a result of the declaration of rights. The mulattoes staged an unsuccessful revolt in 1791, led by Vincent Ogé. The revolt was put down and Ogé was executed.

The failed mulatto revolt was followed by an uprising of slaves on Saint Domingue who had also heard news of the French Revolution. You can see a scene from this revolt in Source 14. On the 22nd August 1791, a voodoo priest named Boukman gathered with the other leaders of the revolt at a secret meeting place in the mountains. They used voodoo chants to signal that their revolt had begun. You can read a translation of their chants in Source 15.

Look at Source 14.

1 Who seems to be winning the fighting here?

2 What weapons do the slaves have?

3 What does the story of this revolt tell us about the slaves' ability to organise themselves?

4 Do you think the slave revolt in Saint Domingue will be permanently successful? Explain your reasons.

SOURCE 14
The planned slave uprising which broke out in Saint Domingue in 1791. The slaves made various demands to improve their conditions, including three free days a week.

'The god of the white man inspires him with crime, but our god calls upon us to do good works. Our god, who is good to us, orders us to revenge our wrongs. He will direct our arms and aid us. Throw away the symbol of the god of the whites, who has so often caused us to weep, and listen to the voice of liberty, which speaks in the hearts of us all.'

SOURCE 15
A translation of the voodoo chants used by Boukman and his followers.

The birth of a black state

Toussaint drew up a new CONSTITUTION for Saint Domingue in 1801. It declared that he was governor of the colony and gave him the right to name his successor. He also set up a system for passing laws without the approval of the authorities in France. The new constitution abolished slavery and banned racial discrimination in the new government.

Toussaint sent a copy of his constitution to Napoleon Bonaparte who had seized power in France in 1799; he is pictured in Source 20. Napoleon was angry that Toussaint had taken control of the colony from him. He also wanted to bring back slavery. So, in 1802 Napoleon sent General Leclerc and French troops to DEPOSE Toussaint and restore slavery to Saint Domingue.

SOURCE 21
A portrait of Henri Christophe.

Toussaint's capture

When Leclerc arrived, he tried to land at Cap Français. He was met by resistance from Henri Christophe, one of Toussaint's most trusted generals, see Source 21. Christophe used 'scorched earth' tactics, burning the town as he retreated inland with his troops. When Leclerc finally landed, he managed to persuade Christophe that the future of the colony would be more secure under French control.

After Christophe transferred his support to Leclerc, Toussaint was captured and sent to France. As he boarded the ship he pledged that the fight for black freedom was not over. You can read part of his speech in Source 22.

SOURCE 20
Napoleon Bonaparte's empire covered much of Western Europe. He also wanted to bring the French colonies under his control.

'In overthrowing me, they have felled in Saint Domingue only the trunk of the tree of Negro liberty; it will shoot forth from the roots, because they are deep and numerous.'

SOURCE 22
An extract from Toussaint's pledge when he was deported to France in 1802.

Independence

The French army soon suffered heavy losses through disease. Leclerc himself died from yellow fever. His successor, General Rochambeau, was a brutal man and there was widespread bloodshed under his regime. The black generals who had fought for Toussaint joined forces with the mulatto leaders against Rochambeau.

The black and mulatto generals placed themselves and their troops under the command of Dessalines (see Source 23). Dessalines led a successful campaign and the French efforts under Rochambeau to regain Saint Domingue failed. To mark his victory, Dessalines tore out the white from the French tricolor flag of red, white and blue. The new flag bore the words 'liberty or death'. The French name of Saint Domingue was changed to Haiti which was the original native American name for the island. Haiti was therefore the first independent black state to be created after a successful slave rebellion.

SOURCE 23
A rare drawing of Dessalines, produced in Germany.

> 1 What do you think of the part played in this story by: Napoleon; Henri Christophe; Dessalines?
>
> 2 Why is Toussaint L'Ouverture regarded as a hero?
>
> 3 Haiti is only one part of one Caribbean island. Why do you think events there had such a big effect on the whole of the Americas?

Struggles after independence

Struggles for power continued even after independence. In 1806 Dessalines was assassinated and the country fell into civil war. Christophe led the north of the country during the conflict. He appointed himself as king and created princes, dukes and barons. He built strong defences and fine palaces, one of which you can see in Source 24.

SOURCE 24
One of the palaces which was built for Henri Christophe. It was known as the 'Palace of Sans Souci'.

NEW SPAIN

FLORIDA

CUBA SANTO DOMINGO
PUERTO RICO

Caribbean Sea

• Caracas

Atlantic Ocean

Bogota •

VENEZUELA

NEW GRANADA

Lima •

PERU

Pacific Ocean

RIO DE LA PLATA

CHILE

Spanish colonies in the
Americas at the end of
the 18th century

0   1500
   km

SOURCE 25
The Spanish empire in the
Americas at the end of the 18th
century.

SOURCE 26
This mansion in Florida is a fine
example of Spanish architecture. It
is a reminder that Florida was part of
the huge Spanish empire in the
Americas.

The end of the Spanish empire

The massive Spanish American empire sprawled over 10 million square kilometres and two continents. Its colonies stretched from the Antarctic Ocean to the North American continent (see Source 25). Today Spanish is still spoken in most South American countries. There are reminders of the Spanish empire in the architecture and customs of many parts of the Americas (see Source 26).

The Spanish colonies could not be shielded from the revolutionary ideas of the late 18th century. When they saw a small country like Haiti winning and keeping its independence, these colonies wondered if they could do the same.

A taste of freedom

In 1807, King Ferdinand VII of Spain was deposed by Napoleon. The Spanish American colonies refused to accept Napoleon's brother, Joseph, as their king. They began to make their own decisions and act as if they were independent. When Ferdinand VII regained his throne in 1815, he set about restoring the American colonies to his control. The colonists had grown to like their independence and did not want to give it up. The wealthy whites supported the king, but the creoles and others joined the independence movement. They called for greater political and economic power for the majority.

SOURCE 27
An early 19th century portrait of Simon Bolivar.

Independence

Bolivar returned to South America and captured the city of Bogota in Colombia in 1819. By 1821 he was in control of a vast area of northern South America, including Venezuela, Colombia and Ecuador. Three years later he signed treaties of alliance with Peru, Mexico, Panama and Argentina. He helped many South American countries on the road to independence and became known as 'The Liberator'. He is still remembered in South America today, see Source 28.

---

1 Why were empires so important to European countries?

2 If you were at school in South America today, which do you think you ought to study?

- the influence of Spain on the history of South America
- Simon Bolivar and South America since independence.

Give reasons for your answer.

Simon Bolivar

Simon Bolivar (pictured in Source 27) was born in 1783 to a wealthy creole family. He went to Europe in 1799 and was caught up in the excitement of revolutionary France. On returning to South America in 1807, Bolivar was shocked to see how the revolutionary ideals of justice and liberty were ignored. He decided to fight for these ideals for the whole of South America.

In 1811, Bolivar declared Venezuela an independent republic. The Church and a strong Spanish army resisted Bolivar and the new republic survived only for a year. Bolivar invaded Venezuela again in 1813 and was defeated a year later. In 1815 he fled to the Caribbean and was given money and support by Alexandre Pétion, the president of Haiti.

SOURCE 28
This statue of Simon Bolivar is in Venezuela.

Struggles for freedom

Slavery and the American Revolution

AIMS

This unit tells the story of the slaves of the USA. Black people played their part in the winning of independence for the USA in 1783, but slavery remained.

White and black Americans struggled for the abolition of slavery. As we shall see, however, it took a Civil War, 1861 to 1865, before this was achieved.

During the 18th century, the 13 American colonies became more and more resentful of British control. Free blacks made up a sizeable minority in the northern colonies – for example about 1,000 of the 15,000 people in Boston in 1770 were black. There were a number of violent riots before the outbreak of the War of Independence in 1775. In 1770 British soldiers killed five rioters in Boston, see Source 1. Black people were among those demonstrating. One of the men shot, Crispus Attucks, was a runaway mulatto servant who had escaped from his owner in 1750. During the war itself, over 5,000 black people, slaves and free, fought for American independence. Some slave-owners sent their slaves to war instead of going themselves. There were four all-black units and one from Massachusetts, the 'Bucks of America', had a black commander.

SOURCE 1
An engraving of the Boston Massacre, 1770.

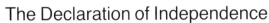

The Declaration of Independence

On the 4th of July, 1776 a Declaration of Independence was adopted. Source 2 is an extract from the declaration, which spelled out the revolutionary ideals of equality and liberty upon which the new nation – the United States of America – was founded. It was drafted by Thomas Jefferson of Virginia and signed by leading colonists, see Source 3.

The War of Independence was a revolution by 13 separate colonies, only temporarily united against the British. When peace came in 1783, each colony still wanted to keep its own independence. It was therefore decided that the UNION of States should allow the greatest possible freedom to local governments.

On the issue of slavery, the attitudes of people living in the more industrial Northern States differed from the attitudes of people from the agricultural South. The South, with its tradition of plantation farming, was not prepared to grant freedom to its slaves. In fact the slave population grew from 700,000 to 4,000,000 between 1783 and 1861. Representatives from the Southern States had put their signatures to the Declaration of Independence, with its promises of equality. In practice, however, they raised several obstacles to the abolition of slavery. It was therefore up to the Northern States to lead the anti-slavery campaign.

'We hold these truths to be self-evident, that all men are created equal, that they are endowed (given) by their creator with certain inalienable rights (rights which cannot be taken away), and that among these are life, liberty and the pursuit of happiness.'

SOURCE 2
The opening section of the Declaration of Independence, which was signed in 1776.

SOURCE 3
This picture, which was painted in 1819, shows the signing of the American Declaration of Independence. You can see Thomas Jefferson holding the document, surrounded by representatives of the 13 colonies.

The Presidents' slaves

Of the first five Presidents of the United States, four were slave owners. George Washington's fine mansion is shown in Source 4, but his slaves lived in such cramped conditions that the children slept on the floor. Thomas Jefferson's slave quarters were comfortable brick houses with proper floors, doors and windows. James Madison boasted that a slave cost him about $12 a year to keep and could earn $257 a year for him.

1 Read Source 2. Do you think Washington, Jefferson and Madison meant what they said in this source?

2 What evidence do you have so far of differences between the North and South in their attitude to black people?

SOURCE 4
The mansion owned by George Washington on his plantation at Mount Vernon, Virginia.

White abolitionists

White abolitionists worked to end slavery mainly because it seemed to conflict with their religious beliefs. Slavery was abolished in the Northern States soon after America declared its independence. In the State of Pennsylvania, where slaves made up about 10 per cent of the population, laws abolishing slavery were passed in 1780.

The Methodist church campaigned against slavery. Its preachers spoke out against the system at religious meetings like the one shown in Source 5. However the real battle for white abolitionists was to change opinion in the Southern States where people were unwilling to end slavery.

SOURCE 5
A Methodist meeting held in 1819.

SOURCE 6
The Wedgwood medallion. It reads 'Am I not a man and a brother?'

ACTIVITY

As it says (above) 'the real battle for white abolitionists was to change opinion in the Southern States'. How would you do this? Write a short article for William Lloyd Garrison's *The Liberator* aimed at Southern slave owners. Remember that many feared their economy would be ruined if they did not have slaves to work on their plantations.

British abolition

Many of the great arguments in the case for abolishing slavery took place in London. Abolitionists in Britain believed that if the slave trade was destroyed, slavery in America and the Caribbean would not survive. In 1787, Thomas Clarkson founded the Society for the Abolition of the Slave Trade. Josiah Wedgwood was one of the early members of this society. He was the owner of a pottery factory. Source 6 shows the medallion he designed which became a popular symbol for the abolition movement.

The transatlantic slave trade was abolished in 1807, but this did not have the crippling effect which the campaigners had hoped for. In fact it resulted in a growth in slave trading within America. There was also a great increase in the kidnapping of free black people who were then sold back into slavery. These new methods made the abolitionists in America more determined in their fight against slavery.

The campaigns

At the forefront of the campaign was William Lloyd Garrison, who is pictured in Source 7. In 1831 he began to print his newspaper *The Liberator*, with the support of black abolitionists. Garrison believed that a national anti-slavery society was needed to combine the efforts of individual states and religious groups. He was encouraged by the success of British abolitionists. In 1833 the British Parliament passed an act to abolish slavery in the British Caribbean, see Source 8.

In December of that year the American Anti-Slavery Society was formed. It started with 60 white and three black members, but within five years its membership had grown to over 250,000 people. The society published its own newsletter to carry the message of emancipation to an even wider audience, see Source 9.

SOURCE 9
An issue of the American Anti-Slavery *Almanac* from 1843.

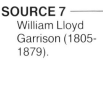

SOURCE 7
William Lloyd Garrison (1805-1879).

SOURCE 8
The abolition of slavery throughout the British Empire is celebrated in Spanish Town, Jamaica on 1 August, 1834.

Black abolitionists

White abolitionists did not bring about the end of slavery on their own. Black people increased their efforts to abolish slavery after the American Revolution. Some of them had fought in the war and gained their freedom in return for military service. Others had escaped from slavery during the war. These men and women had heard the promises of human rights made by Thomas Jefferson in his Declaration of Independence. They wanted such freedoms for all black people. They were prepared to use any way they could to achieve this.

After the American Revolution, free black people in the Northern States began to set up their own churches and build their own places of worship. Richard Allen formed the African Methodist Episcopal Church in 1794. Its first chapel was built at Bethel in Philadelphia. These separate churches allowed black congregations to worship freely. They also became important centres for black communities, and church leaders took an active part in the campaign for abolition. Richard Allen and Absalom Jones, who is pictured in Source 10, founded the Free African Society in Philadelphia in 1793. Members of this society sent a petition to CONGRESS in 1799, demanding an end to the slave trade.

SOURCE 10
This jug, showing a silhouette profile of Absalom Jones, was made in 1808.

Spreading the message

Other black campaigners used the media in their fight against slavery. The first black newspaper devoted to the abolition movement, *Freedom's Journal*, appeared in 1827. It was followed by many others. David Walker was the son of a slave and one of the writers who worked for *Freedom's Journal*. He published his famous *Appeal* against slavery in 1829. You can read an extract from this in Source 11.

Personal accounts

Unlike white abolitionists, black campaigners were able to use their first-hand experiences of slavery to win support for the movement. Some of them wrote moving autobiographies which described their lives as slaves. Sojourner Truth, who you can see in Source 12, escaped from slavery in 1827. She rejected her slave name of Isabella van Wagener and at many meetings she spoke about the suffering and cruelty of slavery. She was also a champion of women's rights. Her demands were not always popular, see Source 13.

Some black abolitionists felt overshadowed and patronised by their white counterparts. Frederick Douglass, an ex-slave from Maryland, felt strongly that black people should be responsible for achieving their own freedom, as you can see in Source 14.

'The greatest riches in all America have arisen from our blood and tears. . . . But Americans, I declare to you, while you keep us and our children in bondage (slavery), and treat us like brutes to make us support you and your families, we cannot be your friends.'

SOURCE 11
An extract from David Walker's *Appeal*, written in 1829.

> **attainment target 1**

1 Use Sources 11, 13 and 14 to explain the attitudes of black abolitionists towards emancipation and their attitudes towards white abolitionists.

2 Why do you think the authors of Sources 13 and 14 felt the way they did?

SOURCE 12
Sojourner Truth who ran away from her master during the 1820s.

We'll have our rights – see if we don't, and you can't stop us from them – see if you can. You may hiss as much as you like but it is coming. I am sitting among you to watch and every once a while I'll come out and tell you what time of night it is.

SOURCE 13
Sojourner Truth spoke these defiant words at the Fourth National Women's Rights Convention in 1853.

'It is emphatically our battle, no one else can fight it for us . . . our relations to the (white) anti-slavery movement must be changed. Instead of depending upon it, we must lead it.'

SOURCE 14
Part of a speech made by Frederick Douglass at a meeting of black abolitionists in 1854.

The Civil War

Abraham Lincoln became President in 1860, see Source 15. By then political leaders in the South knew that the only way they could 'protect' slavery was to break from the union with the Northern States. In December 1860, South Carolina voted to leave the Union. The other Southern States followed, and joined together to form the CONFEDERACY. As you can see from Source 16, the Confederacy was determined to keep slavery.

'Our Confederacy is founded upon the great truth that slavery is (the Negro's) natural and normal condition. This, our new government, is the first in the history of the world based upon this great physical and moral truth.'

SOURCE 16
From a speech made by Alexander Stephens, a Confederate leader, in 1861.

SOURCE 15
A banner used in Lincoln's presidential campaign.

The Proclamation of Emancipation

War between the Confederacy and the remaining States of the Union began on 12th April, 1861. Abraham Lincoln is usually given the credit for giving black slaves their freedom. In fact, although he opposed slavery, he did not see black people as equals. At the beginning of the Civil War, Lincoln declared that the main aim of the fighting was to preserve the Union. Only as the fighting wore on, did slavery become the main issue at stake.

In September 1862, Lincoln issued his Proclamation of Emancipation, promising freedom to all slaves in the Confederate States. He also allowed freed slaves to fight for the Union Army. Altogether, 176,000 black soldiers fought in the Union Army during the Civil War, see Source 17. At first, white officers were reluctant to command black regiments and so they were offered incentives such as free military training, see Source 18. By August 1863, there were 14 black regiments in action on the battlefields and a further 22 regiments in training, see Source 19.

SOURCE 18 ———————●

A free military school for commanders of black regiments.

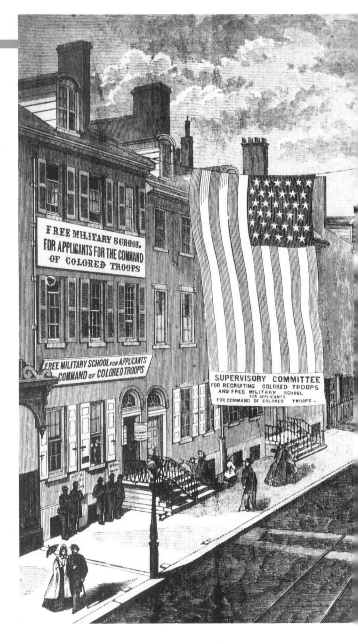

SOURCE 17

'Come and join us brothers': a recruitment poster for black soldiers from the Civil War.

COME AND JOIN US BROTHERS.
PUBLISHED BY THE SUPERVISORY COMMITTEE FOR RECRUITING COLORED REGIMENTS
1210 CHESTNUT ST. PHILADELPHIA.

Black soldiers

The first black fighting unit to be raised was the 54th Regiment of Massachusetts Volunteer Infantry. Under the command of a white colonel, Robert Gould Shaw, the 54th launched an attack on a Confederate fort near Charleston in 1863. Although their assault was beaten back, the black soldiers fought bravely. They earned widespread praise and became the most famous black regiment of the war. Source 20 shows a scene from a feature film which was made recently about the 54th Massachusetts.

Many black people faced prejudice within the Union Army. They were often given weapons and equipment of a poorer standard and did not always have enough supplies of food and medicines. Black soldiers were given lower pay and it was more difficult for them to be promoted to a higher rank.

SOURCE 19

The 107th Coloured Infantry at Fort Corcoran near Washington.

SOURCE 20

A still from 'Glory', a film made about the first black regiment which fought in the Civil War.

attainment target 3

You will need to look at pages 45-47 to answer these questions.

1 What can you tell about the Confederacy (the Southern States) from Source 16?

2 What can you tell about black soldiers in the Union Army from Sources 17, 18 and 19?

3 How useful are Sources 19 and 20 for finding out about black soldiers in the Union Army?

4 Which of Sources 17 and 19 is more useful for finding out about the position of black people in the Union Army?

5 Source 20 is a still from a film made in 1989. Source 19 is a photograph from 1863. Which is the more reliable source for finding out about black soldiers in the Union Army?

6 What would you want to know about Source 20 before using it as evidence for conditions in the 1860s?

7 How reliable is Source 20 as evidence of the position of black people in the USA in 1989?

A free people?

After emancipation

At the end of the Civil War, the South was beaten. In Source 1 you can see a photograph of the destruction of an important Southern town at the end of the war. The future was bleak. The South had built up its wealth from the unpaid labour of a massive slave workforce. These slaves were now free and many of the plantations had been abandoned during the fighting. The cotton empire had collapsed in ruins.

For many black people freedom turned out to be only another kind of slavery. They had hoped that plantations on which they had worked as slaves would be divided equally among them. They looked to the government to do this, but only a small number of slaves were given land from such schemes. In the United States, most of the plantations which had been abandoned during the war were returned to their previous owners. Although some of the freed slaves found jobs in industry, most of them continued to work on the large estates, see Source 2.

Working out a new relationship between former owners and former slaves created many problems. In the British Caribbean islands, the planters were heavily in debt. Before the abolition of slavery, planters measured their wealth by the number of slaves they had. Now they had to find money to pay wages to the men and women they used to own. They could no longer make huge profits. Wages fell, many workers left the plantations and the estates declined.

AIMS

The end of slavery, so long awaited by black people, did not bring them all that they had hoped for. In this unit we shall see that their lives, in the USA and the Caribbean, continued to be difficult. At the same time there were some achievements. You will find out about these and about some of the black heroes and heroines in the continuing struggle for equality.

SOURCE 1

This photograph of ruined buildings in Richmond, Virginia was taken at the end of the Civil War, in 1865.

SOURCE 2
Field workers on a plantation. Most freed slaves returned to the plantations to work for their former owners.

Sharecropping

In the United States, plantation owners did not have the money to pay workers until the crops were harvested. Former slaves had no land to live off, so they agreed to work in return for a share of the crop, see Source 3. The share which workers received was usually one third, but often they had to pay for seed, tools and other expenses out of their share. This system, called sharecropping, continued into the 20th century. It was also used in the Caribbean.

Sharecropping left the ex-slaves with little money. They became dependent on 'country stores' which were run by the planters. The country stores provided them with food and clothing on credit. These then had to be paid for with interest at harvest time. Soon most sharecroppers were tied down with heavy debts.

'Ol' miss and massa (master) was not mean to us at all until after the surrender and we were freed. . . . They got mad at us because we was free and they let us go without a crumb of anything and without a penny and nothing but what we had on our backs. We wandered around and around for a long time. Then they hired us to work on halves (as sharecroppers) and, man, we had a hard time then and I've been having a hard time ever since.'

SOURCE 3
Part of an account written by Frank Fikes, an ex-slave, in the 1930s.

Discuss Sources 1-3 in groups.

1 Which does Frank Fikes (Source 3) prefer: slavery or sharecropping?

2 Does the work which the people are doing in Source 2 look any different from slave labour?

3 Do these sources give us any evidence of improvement in the position of black people after emancipation?

SOURCE 4
A Southern STEREOTYPE of 'the lazy Negro'.

> Every negro who shall be found absent from the residence of his employer after ten o'clock at night, without a written permit from his employer, shall pay a fine of five dollars, or in default therof (if they do not pay), shall be compelled to work five days on the public road, or suffer corporeal (physical) punishment.

SOURCE 5
An extract from the black codes used in the State of Louisiana. They were written in 1865.

Reconstruction

The United States Constitution was amended to make slavery illegal and to give black people the right to full citizenship, including the right to vote. New governments were set up in the Southern States, led by Northerners. During a period known as Reconstruction, these governments tried to rebuild the shattered Southern States. At the same time, they guaranteed civil rights for black people.

The new governments won the support of black voters, but black people gained little political power in their own right. There were no black state governors during Reconstruction. Only in South Carolina, where black people outnumbered white people by a ratio of four to three, did black people manage to achieve a temporary majority in state government.

Southern resentment

All these changes, and the sight of outsiders running their government, were hated by white Southerners. They had not lost the racial prejudice of their slave-owning past, see Source 4. They introduced stiff 'black codes' for their black workers, see Source 5.

By the 1870s, white people had won back control of the Southern States. The position of black people began to get worse. So-called 'Jim Crow' laws were passed. These kept black people out of white schools, restaurants, public transport, hotels and housing. This racial SEGREGATION lasted well into the 1960s.

The Ku Klux Klan

The most sinister response of white racists in the South was the rise of the Ku Klux Klan. This began in Tennessee in 1867 as a secret society, see Source 6. The Klan described itself as an institution of 'CHIVALRY, humanity, mercy and PATRIOTISM'. In fact it was a brutal organisation determined to preserve white supremacy in the South.

The Klan used tactics of violence and intimidation. In 1871 the Ku Klux Klan was reported to have killed 153 black people in one area of Florida alone. The Klan terrorised the South for five years: whipping, LYNCHING, burning and murdering black people. You can read an account written by a victim of the Klan in Source 7.

The Klan in the 20th century

The Klan ceased its terrorist activities in 1873 but in the early 20th century, the Klan emerged again. It attracted a large white, Protestant membership, as you can see in Source 8. This time its victims were Catholics and Jews as well as black people.

SOURCE 6
These two members of the Ku Klux Klan were photographed in 1868.

> attainment target 3

1 What can you tell about Klu Klux Klan meetings from Source 8?

2 What can you tell about the Ku Klux Klan from Sources 6, 7 and 8?

3 Which is the more useful for finding out what the Klan was like in the 19th century, Source 6 or Source 7?

4 Source 4 is a painting. How does that affect its reliability for finding out about
   a black people in the South
   b white attitudes to black people in the South?

5 How can a source be both reliable and unreliable?

'After us coloured folks was considered free and turned loose, the Ku Klux Klan broke out. Some coloured people started farming and gathered old stock. If they got so they made good money and had a good farm, the Ku Klux would come and murder them . . .. There was a coloured man they taken. His name was Jim Freeman. They taken him and destroyed his stuff and him, because he was making some money. They hung him on a tree in his front yard, right in front of his cabin.'

SOURCE 7
This personal account of the activities of the Klan was written by a black victim, Pierce Harper in the 1930s.

SOURCE 8
A mass rally organised by the Ku Klux Klan in 1924.

The Freedmen's Bureau

After the Civil War, Congress knew that the freed black people would face many problems. The Freedmen's Bureau was formed to help them fight these problems. At first, the Freedmen's Bureau worked to improve conditions for black people during the aftermath of the fighting, see Source 9. The Bureau also intended to help black people find work, to offer them education or training, and to provide them with health care.

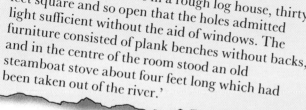

SOURCE 9

This engraving shows black people waiting to receive rations from the Freedmen's Bureau.

'I opened a school here in a rough log house, thirty feet square and so open that the holes admitted light sufficient without the aid of windows. The furniture consisted of plank benches without backs, and in the centre of the room stood an old steamboat stove about four feet long which had been taken out of the river.'

SOURCE 10

This description of a school room for black children was written by their teacher, Elizabeth Bond, in 1864.

Education for black people

As slaves, black people were denied any kind of education. Their owners feared that slaves who could read and write would spread the message of the abolition movement and organise rebellions. During the 1820s and 1830s, all the Southern States passed laws forbidding the teaching of slaves. However, the slaves were hungry for knowledge. Some were taught in secret by other slaves or by sympathetic white masters and mistresses who were prepared to break the law. By the time of emancipation, probably about five per cent of slaves in the South could read and write.

SOURCE 11

These primary school children were photographed in 1899.

The new schools

Freed black people flocked to the new schools which were run by the Freedmen's Bureau. The schools were makeshift: classrooms were set up in the basements of churches, barns, army barracks and other empty buildings, as Source 10 reveals. The schools were overcrowded and had poor equipment. There were not enough books or slates for the children.

In spite of these difficulties, thousands of black children received an education which their parents had been denied a generation earlier, see Source 11. At first nearly all the teachers were whites from the Northern States but by 1870 black people made up about a third of the total number of teachers.

The Tuskegee Institute

Booker T. Washington was born into slavery in 1856 and died in 1915. He struggled to get educated and then became a teacher. He believed that black people needed to be given practical training as well as learning how to read and write. In 1881 he founded the Tuskegee Institute in Alabama, see Sources 12 and 13.

The Tuskegee Institute started with a collection of ramshackle buildings and only 30 pupils. From these humble beginnings, the institute gained a national reputation as one of the largest and finest schools in the South.

SOURCE 12
The Tuskegee Institute, founded in Alabama in 1881.

> **attainment target 1**
>
> 1 In what ways does Source 11 show a change in the lives of black children after the Civil War?
>
> 2 How do Sources 12 and 13 also show change?
>
> 3 From what you have read in this unit so far, how much did the position of black people in the Southern States change after the Civil War?
>
> 4 Were the changes for better or for worse?
>
> 5 How important was the work of the Tuskegee Institute and Booker T. Washington in changing the position of black people in the USA?

SOURCE 13
Black students at the Tuskegee Institute.

SOURCE 14

This painting from 1881 is called 'The Pastoral Visit'. Both family life and religion were important to black people after emancipation.

SOURCE 16

A home for orphaned black children, the Freedmen's Bureau set up many orphanages after the Civil War.

Family life

During slavery, black people were denied the right to a family life. As we have seen, families were often split up when they were shipped from Africa. There was also the risk of relatives being sold to another plantation. Even the work routine, based on long, exhausting shifts, meant that families could spend very little time together. It was not surprising then, that family life was considered very important by the freed slaves, see Sources 14 and 15. However, disruption to families continued after emancipation: many children lost their parents during the Civil War and the Freedmen's Bureau set up orphanages for them, see Source 16.

SOURCE 15

A family of freed black people in Richmond, Virginia, shortly after the Civil War.

Black communities

A strong community spirit developed among black people after emancipation. They joined together in various working clubs for farmers and labourers, in church congregations and in political groups.

Black communities developed their own cultural and social life. African music had survived in the slave spirituals and blues. It also influenced ragtime music. By the end of the 19th century, the mixture of African and western musical traditions produced a new music called jazz. New Orleans became the jazz capital of the United States, see Source 17. In the 20th century jazz has developed in many ways. It has had a powerful influence on rock and roll and pop music all over the world.

SOURCE 17
A jazz club in New Orleans.

SOURCE 18
Frederick Douglass.

A community leader

Frederick Douglass (pictured in Source 18) was one of the few black Americans to become internationally known in the 19th century. He was born on a plantation in Maryland. He knew how slavery broke up families: as a child he witnessed 15 of his relatives being sold to other plantations. He worked for many years as a slave until he ran away to New York city in 1838. British abolitionists bought his freedom for £150 in 1846.

Douglass worked hard for the abolition of slavery (look back at pages 44 and 45). After the Civil War, he was a strong critic of Reconstruction policies. In 1867 he was re-united with his brother, Perry, who had been separated from him for 40 years after having been sold to a different owner.

Douglass travelled to Europe where he gave a series of lectures on black civil rights. He then went on to high office in the USA and in 1889 he was appointed US ambassador to Haiti.

---

1 What does the life of Frederick Douglass tell us about:
   a slavery
   b the struggle for the abolition of slavery
   c black people in the USA after emancipation?

2 We have seen that the lives of most black people in the USA continued to be hard after emancipation, especially in the South. Why were the careers of individuals like Frederick Douglass and Booker T. Washington important at that time?

Breaking free in Jamaica

Conditions for black people in Jamaica hardly improved at all after emancipation in 1833. They had escaped slavery only to become poor, landless, peasants without any political rights. Political control of the colony still rested with the former slave-owning whites and some mulattoes. A series of Acts was passed in the 1830s to prevent black people from getting the right to vote.

It was difficult for black people to make a living from the land, especially during times of drought. As well as facing these hardships, the black population also faced prejudice from the whites. The Governor of Jamaica, Edward John Eyre (pictured in Source 19), was unsympathetic towards the black peasantry, as Source 20 reveals.

'As a whole the peasants of Jamaica have nothing to complain of. . . . They ought to be better off, more comfortable, and more independent than the labourers of any other country. If it is not so, it is due to their own indolence (laziness).'

SOURCE 20
A comment made by Governor Eyre after emancipation was declared in the British colonies in 1833.

SOURCE 19
Governor Edward John Eyre. After the Morant Bay rebellion, Eyre was called back to Britain. Changes were made to the government and laws of Jamaica which improved conditions for black people.

The Morant Bay rebellion

George Gordon was a mulatto who became a successful businessman. He took up the cause of poor black peasants, sold them land and helped to build churches. In the 1850s he went into politics and was elected to the Jamaican House of Assembly. You can see a photograph of the old House of Assembly in Source 21. He attacked Governor Eyre's hostile attitude and warned of the threat of rebellion, see Source 22. Governor Eyre ignored the warning and refused to listen to the complaints of black people.

Paul Bogle, a black Baptist minister, led a rebellion which broke out at the Morant Bay court house in 1865. Over 580 people were killed during the rebellion. Governor Eyre responded by declaring MARTIAL LAW. He arrested Paul Bogle and George Gordon. Both Gordon and Bogle were hurriedly tried and hanged. Today they are national heroes in Jamaica (see Source 23).

SOURCE 21
The House of Assembly where George Gordon spoke out for black rights in Jamaica.

> If we are to be governed by such a governor much longer, the people will have to fly to arms and become self-governing.

SOURCE 22

The warning which Gordon issued to Governor Eyre before the outbreak of the Morant Bay rebellion in 1865.

ACTIVITY

Hold a debate. Choose four members of the class to be Booker T. Washington, Frederick Douglass, Mary Seacole and George Gordon. Each has to make a speech showing why he or she was the most important black person of his or her day. The rest of the class should then take a vote on who they think presented the most convincing case.

SOURCE 23

This statue of Paul Bogle stands in front of the Morant Bay court house in Jamaica.

Mary Seacole

Mary Seacole was born in Jamaica in 1805. Her father was Scottish and her mother was a free black woman. Even when she was a child, she knew that she wanted to be a nurse and her mother taught her all about herbal medicine. When the Crimean War broke out in 1853, she asked to go there to nurse the British soldiers. She was refused by Florence Nightingale and the British War Office, but she went anyway, paying her own fare.

Her services to the men at the front (described in Source 24) were never forgotten. When she got into financial difficulties later, soldiers who had fought in the Crimea organised a music festival to raise money for her. There were over 1,000 performers, nine military bands and an orchestra. She died in 1881 and was buried in Saint Mary's Cemetery, London.

'A more tender or skilful hand about a wound or a broken limb could not be found amongst our best surgeons . . . I have already borne testimony to (shown examples of) her services to all who needed them . . . and I trust that England will not forget one who nursed her sick, and who sought out her wounded to aid and succour (help) them.'

SOURCE 24

Part of a report written by William Russell who was the war correspondent for *The Times* newspaper during the Crimean War (1853-1856).

Black nationalism

After emancipation, black people had to fight on their own to gain equality and respect in society. An important part of this struggle was the growth of BLACK NATIONALISM. White slave-owners had often justified slavery by arguing that it rescued slaves from BARBARISM. Black nationalists proclaimed that African civilisation and tradition was far from barbaric. Black Americans, they said, should show their pride in their common African roots. Dr Edward Blyden wrote a powerful book on this subject in 1908. It was called *African life and custom.* He was born in the Caribbean but moved to Liberia in Africa after it became an independent state in 1847.

Perhaps the most ambitious black nationalist was Marcus Garvey, see Source 25. He was born in Jamaica and moved to the United States where he founded the Universal Negro Improvement Association in 1914. By 1916, the organisation had 1,120 branches in 40 countries. He celebrated the glory of being black and gained a huge following. He wanted to create a great black nation in Africa and encouraged black Americans to return to Africa. He even invested in a fleet of ships, which he named the Black Star Steamship Line, to transport black Americans to Africa. Garvey's vision of a great African state united black people and made them proud of their race and origins. His ideas were taken up by civil rights leaders in the 1960s.

Pan-Africanism

The first Pan-African conference was organised in London in 1900. The Pan-African movement shared many of Garvey's ideas and it worked to improve conditions for all people of African descent. You can read the aims of the movement as set out at the London conference in Source 26.

Through the efforts of leaders like Garvey and Blyden, black people were given a sense of purpose and a shared identity. However they also needed to have national organisations which would work to improve conditions and achieve equality for black people. A number of such organisations were formed at the beginning of the 20th century. In 1900 Booker T. Washington founded the National Negro Business League which provided business aid for black people, see Source 27. Three years later, the National Afro-American Council was formed to protest against discrimination.

- 'To secure to Africans throughout the world true civil and political rights.
- To ameliorate (improve) the conditions of our brothers on the continents of Africa, America and other parts of the world.'

SOURCE 26
The goals of the Pan-African movement.

SOURCE 25
Marcus Garvey, 1887-1940.

SOURCE 27
This photograph of the leaders of the National Negro Business League was taken in 1900. Booker T. Washington is seated in the front row, second from the left.

SOURCE 28
W. E. B. Du Bois gave up his academic career to become the editor of *The Crisis*, the journal for the National Association for the Advancement of Coloured Peoples.

W. E. B. Du Bois

W. E. B. Du Bois, who is pictured in Source 28, was born in 1868 in Massachusetts. He was a brilliant student and the first black person to be awarded a PhD degree from Harvard University. He was determined to bring an end to the racial prejudice which black people had to face in their daily lives. In 1905 he gathered with about 30 black leaders at Niagara Falls and formed the Niagara Movement. It was later re-named the National Association for the Advancement of Coloured Peoples (NAACP), see Source 29. In Source 30 you can read the aims of the movement which demanded civil rights, job opportunities, education and the right to vote for black people living in the United States.

SOURCE 29
The leaders of the Niagara movement which later became the NAACP, photographed in 1905. They believed that black people should be given 'every single right' that white Americans enjoyed.

'The negro race in America . . . needs help and is given hindrance, needs protection and is given mob-violence, needs justice and is given charity, needs leadership and is given cowardice and apology, needs bread and is given a stone. The nation will never stand justified before God until these things are changed.'

SOURCE 30
Part of the statement issued by the leaders of the NAACP in 1905.

Towards a new future

After the First World War, farming in the USA faced bad times. Many black people moved to the industrial cities of the North. Here they found almost as much racial prejudice as in the South, and were hit by the DEPRESSION of the 1930s. Even black soldiers in the US forces in the Second World War were not treated equally.

Black people continued to be denied the rights which had been called for by the NAACP in 1905. It was only in the 1960s that the civil rights movement in the United States, under the inspiring leadership of Martin Luther King, brought hopes of real equality to black people.

1 Do you think the aims of the NAACP (Source 30) accurately state the position of black people in the USA in 1905?

2 Working in pairs, try to find examples from the television and newspapers of today of the things the NAACP called for in 1905: 'help, protection, justice, leadership, bread'. Can you find examples from today's television and newspapers of black people receiving 'hindrance, mob-violence, charity, cowardice, hunger'?

3 How strongly do black people in your class feel a link between themselves as black people in Britain and black people elsewhere in the world?

Glossary

Abolitionists
The men and women who campaigned to bring an end to slavery.

Artefacts
Tools, weapons and utensils which are found by archaeologists. Historians often use artefacts to help them understand how people lived in the past.

Assayers
People who test metal objects to find out what they are made of and whether they are valuable or not.

Auction
A public sale where the goods are sold to the person who bids the highest price. Slaves were sold at auctions in Europe and in the Americas.

Barbarism
An absence of civilisation and culture.

Black nationalism
A movement which developed at the beginning of this century and encouraged black people in the Americas to be proud of their African origins and heritage.

Bolls
The round seed-heads of the cotton plant.

Charter
An official royal agreement which grants certain rights to a company.

Chivalry
A word which was originally used to describe the ideal behaviour of knights in the Middle Ages. Members of the Ku Klux Klan called themselves knights and included 'chivalry' in their motto. This shows how the meaning of words can be twisted to serve the aims of those who use them.

Chronicler
A person who records events in the order that they happen.

Colonization
From the 15th century onwards, people from Europe settled in the countries of the *New World*. The colonization of the New World meant that countries there were given new names and governed by Europeans. The men and women who moved to the New World were called colonists and the places they settled in were called colonies.

Confederacy
The name given to the group of Southern States which supported slavery and fought to preserve it during the Civil War.

Congress
The ruling body of the United States which is made up of the House of Representatives and the Senate. Congress is responsible for passing laws.

Conquistadors
The name given to the Spanish soldier-explorers who led their armies to conquer the native peoples of the Americas.

Constitution
A formal document which lists the rights of a country's citizens.

Depose
To remove someone from power.

Depression
A period of economic hardship and high unemployment which hit many countries during the 1930s.

Fraternity
This means sharing a common interest. Fraternity was one of the aims of the French Revolution.

Hispaniola
The Spanish name given by Columbus to the island which is now divided into Haiti and the Dominican Republic. Columbus first landed on Hispaniola in 1492.

Islamic Empire
Islam spread from its beginnings in 7th century Arabia to influence a vast territory stretching from the borders of China to the Atlantic Coast of Spain. This empire was ruled by *Muslim* governments.

Liberty
Freedom. One of the aims of the French Revolution.

Lynching
A form of mob violence used by the Ku Klux Klan. Victims were accused of an offence and they were then punished or even killed without being given a fair trial.

Maroons
Runaway slaves who escaped from their plantations and set up their own communities in remote places.

Martial law
A system of very strict laws which are usually enforced by an army after a period of rioting or unrest.

Missionaries
Men and women who give religious teaching to people in other countries. During the *colonization* of the *New World*, the church sent many missionaries to convert the native peoples of the Americas to Christianity.

Moors
Muslim people from North Africa.

Mulattoes
People who have one *Negro* and one white parent.

Muslims
People who follow the faith of Islam. Muslims worship Allah – the One True God – and try to live according to the teachings of the Qur'an and the example set by the Prophet Muhammad.

Negro
A member of any of the dark-skinned native peoples of Africa and their descendants in other parts of the world.

New World
Another name for the Americas.

Obeah
A kind of witchcraft which originated in West Africa and was used by *Negroes* in the Caribbean.

Overseers
People who were employed by *plantation* owners to give orders to the slaves. Overseers were usually whites or *mulattoes*.

Patriotism
This word means devotion to your country. However its meaning changed when it was used in the motto of the Ku Klux Klan. Their idea of patriotism was to intimidate black people in order to maintain white superiority.

Plantations
Very large farms on which crops such as *sugar-cane*, tobacco, rice and cotton were grown. Plantations used slave labour.

Segregation
Separation. Racial segregation laws were passed in the Southern States of the USA after emancipation and kept black people out of certain public places which became reserved for whites.

Shilling
A British coin used in the 17th century. There were 20 shillings in a pound and each shilling was divided into 12 pence. This system was used until 1970 when our present decimal currency was introduced.

Stereotype
An unreal (and sometimes unfair) description or image of people based on half-truths, generalisations or prejudice, rather than on fact.

Sugar-cane
The plant from which sugar is extracted. Sugar-cane grows in tropical climates and the plants can reach up to 5 metres in height. The sugar is stored in the stem of the plant.

Union
Another name given to the United States of America when it was founded after the American War of Independence. The Union was also the name for the Northern States in the Civil War which fought against the *Confederacy* of Southern States.

Voodoo
A religious cult originally from West Africa which involves witchcraft. It was common among *Negroes* in the Caribbean during slavery, and is still practised today.

Index

Page numbers in **bold** refer to illustrations/captions

abolitionists 28, 41-44, 55
Allen, Richard 44
artefacts 9-10
auctions 10, 15, **15**

Barbados 18-19, **18-19**, **22**, 24
black nationalism 58-60
Bogle, Paul 56, **57**
Bolivar, Simon 'The Liberator' 39, **39**
Bonaparte, Napoleon 36, **36**, 38
Boukman 33
branding 12, 15, 23, **23**

Caribbean 8, 13, 48-49, 56-57
    slaves 18-19, 22, 28-32, 43
Christian church 7, 16-17, **17**, 22-23,
    26-27, 39
Christophe, Henri **36**, 36-37
class structure 24, **24**, 26, 32
colonies,
    British 14, 22-24, 29-30, 35, 40-
        41, 48
    Dutch 29
    French 14, 23, 32, 35-36
    Portuguese 12
    Spanish 11-12, 13, 17, 38-39
colonization 6-15
Columbus, Christopher 6-9
Cortés, Hernán, 11, **11**
cotton plantations 14, 20-21, 48
creoles 25, 38, 39
Cudjoe 31
culture 26, 30, 55

Dessalines 37, **37**
Diaz, Bartholemew 6
Douglass, Frederick 44, **45**, 55, **55**
Du Bois, W. E. B. 59, **59**

education 25, 52-53, 59
emancipation 43, 46-47
Eyre, Edward John **56**, 56-57

family life 10, 22, **54**, 54-55
free slaves 24-25
Freedmen's Bureau **52**, 52-54
French Revolution effects 33-37

Garvey, Marcus 58, **58**
Gould Shaw, Robert 46

Haiti see Saint Domingue
Hawkins, John 13, **13**
Hispaniola 9, 17
human rights 22, 44, **45**, 59

indentured servants 24
independence 36, 37-39, 41
Indians see native Americans

Jamaica 27, 29-31, **30-31**, 35, **43**,
    56-57
Jefferson, Thomas 41, **41**, 44
Jones, Absalom 44, **44**

kidnapping 29, 42
King, Martin Luther 60
Kofi 29
Ku Klux Klan 51, **51**

Las Casas, Bartolomé de **12**, 17, **17**
laws,
    abolition of slavery 42, 43
    'black codes' 50
    Code Noir 23
    education of slaves 52
    Fugitive Slave Act 29
    'Jim Crow' 50
    Laws of Burgos 16
    Saint Domingue 36
    US Constitution 50
Leclerc, General 36-37
Lincoln, Abraham 45, 46
Lloyd Garrison, William 43, **43**
L'Ouverture, Toussaint **34**, 34-36

maroons 30-31, **30-31**
Martellus, Henricus 6, **7**
Methodist church 42, **42**, 44
Mexico **9**, 11, 39
middle passage **13**, 14-15, **28**
Moors 7, **7**, 10, 16
Mortant Bay rebellion 56-57
mulattoes 25, 33-37
music 27, 55
Muslims 7

native Americans 8-11, 12, 16-17
Negroes 7, 9, 11, 17

obeah 27

Pan-African movement 58
Pinney, John **18**, 24, **24**
plantations 14, 17-24, **21**, 32, 48-49,
    49
Portugal 6-7, 9, 10, 12
Puerto Rico 11
punishment 10, 17, 23, 28, 30

racism 22, 24, 36, 50-51, 59-60
rebellions 28-37, 40, 56-57
religion 7, 16-17, 42-44, 51
    of slaves 23, 26-7, 33
Rochambeau, General 37
Royal African Company 14, **15**, 19

Saint Domingue **32**, 32-37, 39
schools **52**, 52-3
Seacole, Mary 57
sharecropping 49
slavery 10-47
    conditions 14, 21-23, 41, 49-50
    foundations 10-12
    freedom struggles 40-47
    opposition 28-29
    ships 14, **15**, 28
society 24, 26, 32
soldiers, black 7, 11, 44, 46-47,
    46-47, 60
    slave regiments 35, 37, 40
Sonthonax 34
South America 8, 10, 38-39
Spain 6-7, 9, 11, 38-39
sugar plantations 14, 18-19, 24

Tacky 29
tobacco plantations 14
trade 7, 9, 12, 32
triangular trade **13**, 13-14, 19
Truth, Sojourner 44, **45**
Tubman, Harriet 29
Turner, Nat 29
Tuskegee Institute 53, **53**

Underground Railroad 29
United States of America 29, 41
    Civil War 45-48
    Depression 60
    freedom struggles 40-47
    Reconstruction period 50-51, 55

voodoo **26**, 27, **33**
voting rights 56, 59

Walker, David 44
wars, 7, 35, 37, 40-41, 45-48
Washington, Booker T. 53, 58, **59**
Washington, George 41
Wedgwood, Josiah 42, **42**
West Africa 7-10, 12

Ximenes, Cardinal **16**, 17

First published in 1992 by CollinsEducational
77-85 Fulham Palace Road
Hammersmith
London
W6 8JB

ISBN 0 00 327241-9

Cover designed by Glynis Edwards
Book designed by Don Parry, Peartree Design Associates
Series planning by Nicole Lagneau
Edited by Helen Mortimer
Picture research by Caroline Mitchell
Artwork by Julia Osorno (unit motif artwork and pages 4, 5, 24) and VAP Group Ltd (pages 6, 8, 13, 32, 38)
Production by Mandy Inness

Typeset by Dorchester Typesetting Group Ltd

Printed and bound by Stige-Arti Grafiche, Italy

Acknowledgements

Every effort has been made to contact holders of copyright material, but if any have been inadvertently overlooked the publishers will be pleased to make the necessary arrangements at the first opportunity.

Photographs The publishers would like to thank the following for permission to reproduce photographs on these pages:

T = top, C = centre, B = bottom, R = right, L = left

Abby Aldrich Rockefeller Folk Art Collection 27; American Antiquarian Society 46T; Barbados National Trust 18, 22,/Sunbury House 19C; Bridgeman Art Library 3, 19T&B; Bristol Museums and Art Gallery 24; British Library 43T; British Museum 7T, 14C; Chicago Historical Society 15C, 46B, Corcoran Gallery of Art 54T; Culver Pictures 49, 54C; Derbyshire Archaeological Society/The Arkwright Society 20R; Mary Evans Picture Library 33T; Werner Forman Archive 9, 12B; Friends Historical Library, Swarthmore College 43C; Giraudon 35T (Anne Louis Girodet-Trioson), 36B (Lauros-Giraudon, Jacques Louis David); Robert Harding Picture Library 16R, 39B, 55T; Rutherford B. Hayes Library 51L; Hulton Picture Company 47T, 54B, 55C, 59B; Hutchison Library 10B, 26T&B, 37R; Jamaican Tourist Board 57; Library of Congress 25T, 42T, 48, 51R, 52T, 53, 59T; Mansell Collection 12T, 14B, 20B, 28R, 30B, 31C, 34C, 37L, 43B, 56T; MAS 7B, 16L, 17B, 39T; Museo de America, Madrid 10T, 11; Museum of Fine Arts, Boston 28L; Museum of Modern Art, New York 52B; National Maritime Museum 13, 15; National Gallery of Art, Washington, Rosenwald Collection 40; National Graphics Center 41C; National Library of Jamaica 31T, 56B; National Portrait Gallery, Washington/Art Resources NY 44; New Hampshire Historical Society 45B; New York Historical Society 21C; Popperfoto 58; Roger-Viollet 32B, 33C, 34T, 35B, 36T, Ann Ronan Picture Library 20L; Royal Commonwealth Society 23T; Schomberg Center for Research in Black History (New York Public Library) 60; Sophia Smith Collection, Smith College 45T; Tristar Pictures 47B; Virginia Museum of Fine Arts, Richmond 25B (gift of Miss Dorothy Payne), 29L (Paul Mellon Collection); Wilberforce House/Hull City Museums 23B; Wadsworth Atheneum 50; Trustees of the Wedgwood Musem, Barlaston, Staffordshire 42C; ZEFA 17T, 30T, 38, 41B.

Cover photograph: Bridgeman Art Library

The author and publishers gratefully acknowledge the following publications from which written sources in this book are drawn:

Africa World Press, Inc. for extracts from Jan Carew, *Fulcrums of Change*, 1988; Random House, Inc. for an extract from C.L.R. James, *The Black Jacobins*, 1963.